The Crown
Without
The Conflict

The Crown
Without
The Conflict

By
Linda and David Jamison

For additional copies please contact:
    Linda Jamison
    1-208-525-8235

For up-to-date contact information search for
ISBN 1-59971-073-0 on the following website:
http://www.isbn4authors.com/database/index.php

Cover Design:
    Allen Haroldsen

ISBN: 1-59971-073-0

Acknowledgements

There are reasons to remain silent: the pain of sharing personal experience and the need for privacy. If not for the encouragement of friends, these justifications would have silenced us. After writing some of my experience I felt more than ever, it was too personal to share. Then came the female touch.

Women are more open to talking and sharing personal experiences than most men. Linda talked to **Janet Smiley** who called two weeks later on the evening of October 15, 2003, and said, "Linda, I've got to tell you that a strong impression came to me three times today that your story needs to be told. It is very powerful and has the potential to help many people . . ." I listened to Linda recount this with interest but was still unconvinced. Later Linda related our story to **Janet Hoover**. Janet said, "Hearing this story makes me not want to give up." Now with encouragement from two sources I realized we grow through each other's experience.

Linda and I collaborated on this story, each writing portions of it. Our primary thanks goes to each other. Without Linda's persistence this story would still be only a personal one.

We also give thanks to **Catherine** and **Mark Croft**, **Marilyn Potter**, **Annette Christiansen** and others who share experiences, a poem and a song in the book.

Then to **Marie Creager**, **Linda Robertson** and **Maryia Roberts** for their editing skills; and to **Belinda Willis**, **Mike Palmer**, **Maggie Croft**, **Cindy Quinn**,

Karen Batt, Dixie Johnson, Veldon Hix, Susan Grover, and **Cathy Housley** for proofreading.

Thank you to the many friends and family who read our story in its developing stages, **Brenda Stegelmeier, Carla Campbell, Faith Palmer, Jay Dye, Helen Ferguson, Jody James, Deann Colling, Anita Burke, Rosalie Jamison, Al** and **Ida Arave, Craig** and **Diane Hall, Arlene Hix, Heather Mielke, Lori Ramsey, Maryan Holloway, Anita Haire** and **Chad Daybell.** Your positive feedback was vital to our story's completion.

Thank you to **Belinda Willis** for the red wagon photograph on the front cover, and to **Faith Palmer** for the cemetery photograph on the back cover.

Thank you to **Garna Mickelsen** for the back cover summary.

A special Thank you to **Allen Haroldsen** for his cover design. Allen is a local artist and friend whose portfolio includes the sculpting of the Nauvoo Temple sunstones.

Dedicated
to
Vaughn and Aisha Jamison

Table of Contents

Prologue

David and I met in high school, but not until the last month of our senior year (Skyline's class of '79) while on a seminary trip to Salt Lake City. We were touring Hogle Zoo. It was while standing in front of the elephant cage to be exact, that I first spoke to my future husband.

I was standing twenty feet away when I overheard David say to his friend Chris, "I don't think I've ever really seen an elephant before." I had lived in Beaverton, Oregon, during my childhood and had many chances to see elephants at the Portland Zoo. I was curious and wanted to know what David was thinking. David says he noticed me when I got on the bus that morning before leaving Skyline, and wondered, "How can I meet her?" Then, there I was asking him, "You've never seen a live elephant?"

I don't remember the rest of that conversation, only that we wanted to ditch his friend Chris, real fast. We spent the rest of the time at Hogle Zoo together. We separated before getting back on the bus for lunch. As I walked past the peacocks I had a strong premonition that this guy I had just met was going to be my husband.

After touring Temple Square, David asked me to sit with him on the way home. Chris, who had been sitting with David, came on the bus and stopped dead for a moment with a "So that's how it's going to be!" look on his face and walked on by to the back of the bus.

When we got as far north as the Malad pass, David started telling me about his grandparents, Reed and Maggie Jamison, who lived just over that hill in Franklin,

Idaho, east of Malad. It turns out that my grandparents also lived over that hill.

My mother's parents, Leonard and Eleanor Hobbs, lived at the north base of Little Mountain in Franklin, Idaho. My dad's parents, Ingram and Lorene Smith, lived in Preston, six miles north of Franklin. Preston has become a famous small town. The movie *Napoleon Dynamite* was filmed in Preston. The house doorstep that Pedro puts the cake on is my Uncle Larry's. Uncle Larry's house sits only half-a-mile east of the original Leonard Hobbs homestead where my mother grew up.

Every summer, during the years we lived in Oregon, my parents brought us to Preston. My favorite part of the trip was when we visited Uncle Larry's dairy farm in Franklin and played with my cousins. We always sat around the big classic red and white tiled farm kitchen with its white metal cupboards telling stories. One of the things I'll never forget them telling us was how good tuna fish and homemade raspberry jam sandwiches tasted (comparable in taste to turkey with cranberry sauce). Besides laughing at stories in the farmhouse kitchen, we spent a lot of time playing in the hayloft, building forts and swinging on the rope.

The Jamisons, Smiths and Hobbs all knew each other. My Grandpa Ingram Smith and Reed Jamison were friends way back in the early 1900's. Grandpa always referred to Reed as a, "Prince of a fellow." Reed and Maggie Jamison, and Leonard and Eleanor Hobbs are all buried in the Franklin cemetery.

David's mother, Rosalie, is an Arave from Taylor, Idaho, which is why David's parents ended up in Idaho

Falls. My parents left Cache Valley, and moved to Idaho Falls after Grandpa Smith moved here in the 1950's to sell trailers for Max Seagle Motor Homes.

Almost four years after high school David and I were married in the Idaho Falls Temple on February 19, 1983. David had served a two-year mission in Sweden. And I had attended two years at Ricks College and one year at BYU Provo.

In August of 1983 we moved up to Moscow, Idaho, and both enrolled at the University of Idaho. I was able to complete a Bachelors degree in education. I have a K thru 12 teaching certificate in Physical Education and English that I have never used in the public schools and has long ago expired.

Kids came along starting March 7, 1986, with the birth of our first child, Daniel Reed, in Moscow, Idaho. David got a start on his electrical engineering degree at the U of Idaho but due to financial problems decided to leave Moscow and move to Rexburg where he completed a two-year Electronics Engineering Technology degree in one year with excellent grades.

In late February of 1987 we were offered a job as house parents for a small group of developmentally disabled women. Beth and Max Sargent were the owners of this shelter home. I was all too glad to leave our cold basement apartment in Rexburg and give up my house and window-cleaning jobs to live at Sargent Manor in Idaho Falls. This is how we got our start as care providers. We only had the house-parent job for seven months when David got a job fixing copier machines for Yost's Office Systems in Salt Lake City. Four months after moving to

Salt Lake, Sarah Kay, our second child was born on December 19, 1987.

After one year at Yost's, David got a job at the University of Utah. He became an Apple Certified Technician and repaired the first Apple Computers on the market.

One beautiful Saturday morning in April of 1989, I woke up with a strong feeling that we needed to go for a ride. Not knowing why or where we were supposed to go, we drove south on State Street. When we got to Murray, Utah, David noticed an Apple Computer Store and said, "Should I go see if they have any openings?" I sat in the car with Dan and Sarah while David went into the computer store to apply. He came back to the car with a huge grin on his face. "And guess where the job is?"... Idaho Falls!" I knew the job was David's. I knew we were supposed to go back home. I knew a way was being made for our family.

Alpine Computing paid for us to move to Idaho Falls. We found a two-bedroom apartment on Cottage Avenue. Being pregnant with our third child, Roslyn, I knew our apartment was not going to be adequate for long. We spent the summer of 1989 looking for a house, but with no savings, our efforts were futile.

After one particularly discouraging Saturday of house hunting we ended up at David's parents house to look at their newspaper. I was looking at the job section, and as my eyes scanned down the column I said, "What we need is a way to make some money." By the time I said it my attention was focused on a small add that said, "House parents needed for six adult developmental disabled women…" I just knew it was the shelter home job we had left two years ago. Sure enough, the job was ours again. This time it was owned by Dennis Smith and called Smith Manor.

The next four years were intensely busy. We had two more children, Roslyn Gail, born October 17, 1989, and Isaac Grant, born November 30, 1991.

David continued to work at Alpine Computing until he got his foot in the door at the INEL and was hired as a computer technician in field services in February of 1990.

Besides taking care of the women and my own children, I had a part-time job proofreading depositions for a court reporter. After four years at Smith Manor, David and I were ready for a home of our own.

In February of 1993 David found a "House For Sale by Owner" in the country, north of Idaho Falls. David told me to go take a look at it. I took my mom with me to see it for the first time. No one was living in it at the time so we were unable to see the inside. As I pulled out of the driveway my mother said, "I have the best feeling about this house."

Richard Mole came to Smith Manor with the paperwork for us to sign. Among the many things we talked about with Dick, he told us about his mother's death. I vividly remember him saying to me, "I can tell by the way you are responding that you have never had a death experience." He was right. I was a little bit self-conscious wondering how he could tell that.

After five years in Coltman, life seemed perfect. David had a good job that paid for further college education, and he was making good progress toward his engineering degree. We had been blessed with two more beautiful children Vaughn Joseph, on June 18, 1994, and Aisha Mae on May 10, 1996. We were also care providers for two women.

I remember visit teaching my friend, Julie Buhler, in September of 1998. Julie had just had gallstone surgery. We were talking about her pain and trials in general. I made the comment: "I've never had a major trial in my life…"

The weather on Tuesday May 11, 1999, in Idaho Falls, Idaho, was gorgeous. Billowy white cumulus clouds accented a clear, azure sky. The temperature was perfectly unnoticeable. All day a mild breeze pushed the huge cotton clouds towards Wyoming, our eastern neighbor. On a day like this, from our house on East River Road, I can see the Grand Tetons.

If cumulus clouds rise high into the air and grow dark and heavy they are called cumulonimbus, or "a pile of rain." Little did I know, the beautiful white clouds were literally going to grow dark and heavy, and that the most severe storm of my life was on the horizon.

Preface

When children die young, before an accountable age, they are innocent and receive a crown of exaltation without the conflict of life on earth.

> "The Lord takes many away even in infancy, that they may escape the envy of man, and the sorrows and evils of this present world; they were too pure, too lovely, to live on earth; therefore, if rightly considered, instead of mourning we have reason to rejoice as they are delivered from evil, and we shall soon have them again."[1]

Without a Godlike ability to see our life from beginning to end, we mortals lack perspective. We call accidental deaths tragedies and spend the rest of our lives assembling scattered experiences, searching for a higher understanding that only emerges as the pieces fit together, and the picture on the puzzle of our life begins to appear.

---

[1] Documentary History of the Church 4:517

The Crown Without the Conflict

Chapter 1
The Calm

Linda

When someone you love becomes a memory, the memory becomes a treasure. Our youngest daughter, Aisha Mae Jamison, turned three years old on Monday, May 10. My mother, Aisha's Grandma Smith, had tied a quilt blanket made out of material patterned with little green frogs for her birthday. Mother was anxious to bring the blanket out Sunday evening the 9, instead of waiting for Monday. This happened to be Mother's Day that year. I will be forever grateful for that evening. Aisha loved her blanket. She was wrapped in it and asleep on my lap before Grandpa and Grandma Smith left. After my parents left, I spent the closing hours of Mother's Day rocking my little girl. I don't think I've ever rocked a child longer than I did Aisha that night. This was our last time in the rocking chair together. The memory is more than a treasure. I consider it a divine gift.

On Monday morning, Aisha's birthday, Grandma Smith, my son Vaughn, Aisha and I went shopping. Aisha needed her "main" birthday present, and I was on a quest to find my next quilt pattern and material. JoAnn's Fabric was our first stop. The two short toy aisles at the fabric store did nothing for Aisha. She wanted a dress, a "pretty dress." Her request became so persistent and loud that I abandoned my quilt hunt. A feeling of guilt came over me accompanied by the thought that I should be at the park playing with my children instead of shopping on my daughter's birthday.

We left JoAnn's Fabric and drove straight to Wal-Mart. Grandma Smith and I selected three dresses from which Aisha made the final choice. She chose an adorable spring dress. It was made of seersucker material and had light green and pink stripes that were crisscrossed diagonally against a white background.

Our next stop was the Two Dollar Fabric store on 17th Street. Grandma Smith was also on a quilt material hunt. Mom was making each of her grandkids a tie-quilt for their birthday that year. At this store Mom found some boy fabric: hunter green with Irish setter dogs. Vaughn's fifth birthday was coming next, on June 18. "Do you like this material Vaughn?" asked Grandma. "NO!" Vaughn adamantly replied. Mom bought the dog fabric anyway, which was unlike her. Normally she is overly concerned and asks several times if someone likes his or her gift. Mother didn't realize she would be sewing the fabric into a quilt for our oldest son Daniel, not Vaughn.

After three stores, Mom was out of energy and needed to sit in the van. Vaughn and Aisha sat with her while I ran a few more quick errands. Mom has congestive heart failure, and her heart had been acting up the previous two weeks. While sitting in the van with Grandma, Aisha held up her new dress. With two small fingers holding the brand tag she said, "Does this say, 'Aisha's dress'?" This memory has become one of my mother's most cherished treasures.

Our Last Morning Together

Tuesday, May 11, dawned bright, beautiful and warm, warmer than any day so far that spring, warm enough for the kids to go outside and play! I love mornings and often feel ambitious, but this day my energy level was off the charts. I prayed to get a lot done, to be happy, and to have the Spirit with me.

When my fifth grader, Sarah, called from Fairview Elementary School asking me to bring the sack lunch she had packed and left on the kitchen island, I saw it as an opportunity to multi-task. I hoped my friend, Deann, who lives on the way to the grade school, could do a painting favor for me. I had two wall decorations friends had given me that I wanted to match. I grabbed the small shelf off the front room wall and quickly sanded the top board. The sander was already plugged in on the front deck because sanding the deck was one of about six projects I had going.

On the way home from the school I stopped by Deann's house and gave her the frame and shelf. As I was stepping back down her cement steps I said, "By the way Deann, do you like to quilt?" Her reply was, "Yes, I do; I've done a little bit and would like to do more of it in the future." Then, of all the things she could have chosen to tell me next, she said, "My Father died when I was four. My mother said that if it wasn't for quilting and all her friends, she does not know how she would have made it through his death."

This really left an impression on me. I did not know Deann had lost her dad at such a young age. With my friend's words concerning death still on my mind, I returned home. David left for work soon thereafter and my morning settled into a peaceful, undisturbed calm for the next five hours.

Following a breakfast of peaches, toast and tuna fish, Vaughn and Aisha ended up on my lap in the kitchen rocking chair. I read them a few children's books, and then they were off downstairs to play with toys. Meanwhile I started cutting out a stuffed bear pattern at the kitchen table. It wasn't long before my two toddlers were back upstairs in the brown kitchen rocker, this time fighting over a pile of plastic, primary-colored mega blocks.

Aisha was sitting in the rocker with a large pile of blocks in her lap, trying to protect them with her arms from Vaughn who was standing next to her. I suggested to little sister that she share. Aisha's response caused me to smile. I controlled the urge to laugh as she said, "I want to share with Sarah, and Roslyn and Isaac, and I don't want to share with Vaughn."

We all ended up in the rocking chair again, this time I was trying to satisfy their requests for a certain primary song. These kids liked to sing and did so from time to time. I knew they were enjoying their Sunday singing time at church; this pleased me a lot. They were going to be singers like their dad. I thought it was unusual this morning that both Vaughn and Aisha kept pestering to find a certain primary song. I sang, "Jesus Wants Me for a Sunbeam" and "Jesus Once Was a Little Child." Neither song was the right one.

Their asking turned persistent, exactly like Aisha had acted in JoAnn's fabric on Monday about her dress. Needing help, I went to the stereo cabinet in the front room and found the CD cover of LDS Primary Songs. Looking through the list of song titles did not help. In spite of my best efforts to figure out which song they wanted, what they were asking for just did not sound familiar. I turned on a John Denver CD instead and the primary song was forgotten. To this day, I wonder if the song they wanted to hear held more meaning than I will ever know.

After tuning into "Take Me Home, Country Roads," I decided to take on another project. We had previously built Roslyn, my third child, a shelf for her bedroom. I never did like the long brackets, which stuck out too far and made the shelf look funny. I was going to fix this problem right now, so upstairs I went. I brought the shelf back downstairs to the front room fireplace brick hearth, which made a good workbench.

Vaughn and Aisha were both with me during this project. At one point Vaughn had a hammer in his hand and acted like he wanted to pound on the brick. I gently told him, "Don't hit the brick," and took the hammer away. At this moment I became consciously aware that the Spirit was with me. It had to be! This was not like me to show this much patience with my kids for this long. I was intensely happy.

After dismantling the shelf and shortening the brackets, I decided my dishes needed to be finished. As I stood at the kitchen sink listening to the music, I became emotional and started to cry. I was thinking about my

Mom's heart problem. On October 1, 1996, she fell from my Dad's homemade ladder while picking apples; I've worried about her ever since. I imagined I was speaking at her funeral. The talk I was creating was all about faith.

Loretta Evens, a Relief Society teacher, once said that every mother gives her child at least one gift. My mom's greatest gift to me is faith. I learned to have faith by the way I was raised. The poem "Children Learn What They Live" says that if a child lives with security he learns to have faith. I had security. Everyday when I came home from school and yelled out, "Mom!" she was always there.

Finally the dishes were done and I went back into the front room to reassemble the shelf. It was easy work twisting screws back into the holes as I sat on the brick hearth listening to the music. Song number four "For Baby," touched my spirit. The words and melody of this song really brought on my emotions.

> I'll walk in the rain by your side,
> I'll cling to the warmth of your tiny hand
> I'll do anything to help you understand
> I'll love you more than anybody can
>
> And the wind will whisper your name to me
> Little birds will sing along in time
> Knees will bow down when you walk by
> And morning bells will chime
>
> I'll be there when you're feeling down
> To kiss away the tears that you cry

I'll share with you all the happiness I've found
A reflection of the love in your eyes

And I'll sing you the song of the rainbow
A whisper of the joy that is mine
And knees will bow down, when you walk by
And morning bells will chime

This song perfectly describes the way I feel about my children. I started to cry again, so much so that as I wiped the water from my eyes I thought, "I've got to stop this before someone comes to the house and finds me this way." Little did I know that within one hour, many people really would be coming to my home. Not only would they see my tears, but my shock and anger as well.

The shelf was finished and looked better. While I was upstairs hanging it back on the wall, Vaughn left the house. When I came back downstairs I helped Aisha go to the bathroom. I remember thinking that I had reached some kind of milestone; my baby was now three years old and potty trained! As I helped her finish dressing, I felt an overwhelming love for my little girl who was growing up.

By now it was after 1:00 p.m. I had not eaten since early morning and suddenly felt hungry. The kids had snacked on homemade bread many times since breakfast so I decided to grab a quick lunch of hard crackers, mayo and cucumber slices (something David had been introduced to and enjoyed eating while on his mission to Sweden). Just before I started eating I glanced through the open back door to see Vaughn pulling Aisha in their red Radio Flyer wagon they had received for Christmas.

Pulling that wagon was their most favorite thing in the world to do.

When finished eating I thought, "What should I do next?" A very compelling idea came to my mind, "Mow the lawn." Knowing the grass needed to be removed from around the blade, I went to the kitchen desk and opened the tool drawer to retrieve a chisel, then walked out the front door and down the ramp to the lawnmower sitting in the driveway. Turning the mower on its side, I proceeded to remove built up grass. No more than 90 seconds had passed when Aisha's terrified scream jerked me around to face the most horrific storm of my life.

Chapter 2
The Storm

Thirty yards from where I was kneeling in the driveway sat my father-in-law's old, "fun-time" pick-up truck camper, on blocks and jacks. Thick grayish black smoke was forcefully pouring out every seam of the old crank-style slat windows in the overhang. A column of black smoke had already ascended thirty feet into the sky.

Aisha's scream was very high pitched and loud, yet muffled. Instinctively I knew both Vaughn and Aisha were in there, though I did not see them go in. As I dropped the chisel and started to run, my thoughts were, "How did this happen, this bad, this quick? I was gazing out the big kitchen window just three minutes ago! The camper is in view of that window, yet I saw nothing! When walking down the ramp and while in the driveway-- why didn't I see anything?" I was scared! A heart-pounding adrenaline rush flooded through me.

When I got to the camper, I jumped up on the old cement foundation it was sitting on and flung open the back door, only to be greeted by a wall of lighter gray smoke, heat and silence. I noticed wisps of white smoke were mixed with the gray. The smoke at the back door seemed to be standing still compared to the boiling black smoke at the front of the camper.

Aisha had only screamed once. I could not see her, or anything in the camper through the thick smoke. I started to move my body toward the open door to try to stick my head in, but didn't. Common sense told me it was too dangerous. I remember thinking, "Water hose from the front faucet; No! That's too far away." Then I thought about Riena, my next-door neighbor, "No, she's not home and neither is David!" I have never in my life experienced such extreme terror merged with total helplessness. Panic set in. All I could do was sort of dance or jump around at the back door and scream hysterically. I didn't know what to do. A very clear thought came suddenly to my mind (I've always felt that this thought, though it was not an actual voice, came from a man). The thought commanded me, "Leave them alone, you have four other children to raise."

I was then able to stop screaming and run to the house. I jumped up onto the deck and ran through the open back door, into the kitchen where the portable phone was waiting on my desk. I grabbed the phone, ran back outside, and stood trembling on the deck as I dialed 9-1-1.

The dispatcher came on the line, "911, what is your emergency?" Crying made my first attempt to say, "There is a fire," undistinguishable. The dispatcher said, "Excuse me Ma'am?" Then I screamed, "A Fire! My kids are dead!" Crying also disrupted the dispatcher's second question, "What is the location? -- Ma'am I need your location." With forced self-control I answered, "1-2-7-8-9 North, 5 West." I was hysterical. No less than ten times the dispatcher said things like, "Okay Ma'am, stay with me here; Ma'am stay calm. I need you to stay calm; we've got a lot of help on the way, ma'am. We're talking to them now--they're on their way."

As I stood with a full view from the deck, I watched the smoke filled trailer turn into a spreading inferno. The whole camper, front to back, top to bottom, within one minute, became engulfed in orange and white flames. Seconds more and the wind blown flames caught my neighbor's haystack on fire right through the chain link fencing. The burning haystack then ignited my neighbor's cinder block barn roof. Huge flames were coming out both ends of the barn roof gables. It looked like the flames were also threatening to catch the wooden fence on fire between our house and Carroll's. I screamed to the dispatcher, "My neighbor's house is going to catch on fire!" I knew that if the fence caught fire, so would their house.

Over the next 10 minutes my 911 nightmare continued. As many times as the dispatcher told me to stay calm, I yelled to her that my two children were in the camper burning to death. Most of the time I referred to Vaughn and Aisha as my babies.

When asked, "How old are your children?" My response was, "Three and five. I think they're going to be burned beyond recognition!" I was then asked, "What caused the fire?" I replied, "I don't know; it's not my camper. It's my father-in-law's; it's horrible!"

At this point listening to the dispatch tape, there is a marked decrease in my hysteria, my breathing can be heard and there are a few more seconds of pause before I reply to the dispatcher's questions. From the sky directly south of our deck I was receiving help, literally from heaven. I turned my view away from the fire and looked directly toward the south. As I looked at the white clouds and azure sky the most comforting thoughts were rapidly coming to my mind. I learned that my children really were being called home. They were going for a reason. I wasn't told why. The strong peaceful feeling was very sustaining. When people comment on how strong I was, I need to give credit to the invisible yet literal help I received at this time.

It seemed as if the time on the phone had been forever, and still I could not hear sirens. By now I was in a state of shock. My mouth was dry, and I felt weak enough to collapse. With no energy left to run, I started walking around to the front yard. I wanted to be close to the road to wave down the fire truck. I desperately needed someone and twice told the dispatcher, "I need somebody." I was standing in the driveway under my neighbor's Ponderosa pine tree and realized I could feel Vaughn's and Aisha's presence. I felt that they were above me, next to the branches of the tree. This was comforting even though I couldn't see them.

When I got a few steps closer to the road the dispatcher asked me, "Can you see the trailer now?" "Yes--it's getting worse!" I answered. "Do you have any way to get a hose and go work on it?" "NO, It's TOO BIG! I'd be DEAD." A few seconds later I was yelling, "The thing is collapsing to the ground now…oh jeez….MY BABIES!" This was the worst moment. I didn't think the heart wrenching pain I was physically and emotionally experiencing as I watched the camper burn could get any worse, but when the camper caved in, my horror intensified.

The dispatcher wanted to know, "Is there anyone we can contact to come help you?" "Yes, my husband David, David Jamison. He works at the INEEL, the electric vehicle place. And Miles Carroll, (my next-door neighbor, whose hay and barn were burning) he teaches shop at Idaho Falls High School."

Finally, help arrived. I was still on my cordless phone with the dispatcher when she heard me start to speak with the deputy; "I'm going to go let you talk to the deputy. Okay, go ahead and hang up now," she said.

My first words to the deputy were, "My babies are in there; they're gone." "What were they?" he asked. In amazement, I realized that he might be thinking my "babies" were little ducklings or kittens. In harsh reality I answered, "My CHILDREN, My KIDS!"

I relived this scene many times, for several months, when awakening from sleep. Watching the camper collapse was by far the hardest moment.

Two and one-half years later, I experienced a similar escalation of emotion as I watched the twin towers being destroyed on September 11, 2001. Seeing the planes crash, followed by billowing smoke was bad enough. But when those towers collapsed and you knew all those people were still inside, the anguish I literally felt in my heart intensified beyond anything I have ever experienced, except for on May 11, 1999.

Unbeknownst to me, David wrote a large part of his story two years earlier. He does a remarkable job capturing some of the intensity of our experience. In present tense narrative David will now take you to ground zero.

Chapter 3
Ground Zero

David

I get up on this day as any other and get ready for work. At the top of the stairs I see my little Aisha. She rises earlier than Vaughn and is already up eating her breakfast at the island.

I say to Aisha, "Are you my cute-cute?" She replies, "No, I'm mommy's cute-cute." Linda is pleased that Aisha regards her so. I give Aisha the sad, pouting father look. With a furled, concerned brow she relents, "O.K. I'm both your cute-cute."

I'm surprised and delighted! Aisha is beginning to put sentences together. I give her a kiss, grab my things and go to work. Work is unusual in that there are many things away from my desk that need attention. My phone is very difficult to hear above the constant whir of fans in the noisy lab. Clair, a co-worker, comes and tells me with great concern that the WCC, (Warning Communications Center), is trying to get in touch with me. I ask if she knows what it is in regards to. She says that it has something to do with a camper shell on fire.

I imagine in my mind little Vaughn playing with matches and catching the camper shell on fire. I reassure myself that the camper was old and pass it off as no great loss. I say, "Some little person is going to be in big trouble."

As I walk to the phone, I think to myself, "Linda is probably panicky or just plain mad. I know she has wanted to get that thing off our property." With some humor I think, "Well, I guess that is one way to get rid of the thing."

I call the WCC and become frustrated that the young lady on the other end of the phone will only tell me there is an emergency at home and I need to call there. I remember thinking, "Why would they let Clair know it was a camper shell fire, but not say a word to me?"

I call home; ring, ring, ring, someone finally answers the phone. I'm surprised to hear an unknown voice, and I ask for Linda. They ask, "Is this David?" "Yes." I reply. Linda comes to the phone, and in a voice much worse than expected, says, "David do you know what is happening?"

I say, "Something about a camper shell on fire." Linda says, "Your Dad's camper is burning and Vaughn and Aisha are in it." Pause------"Are they all right?" Frantically: "They're Dead!" "Are you sure?" More frantically: "Yes!"

I'm dazed as if reeling from a powerful blow. I can't believe it. "They're in the shed! They have to be somewhere else. You are mistaken!" I think to myself. I'm tempted for a split second to pass this reassurance on to Linda; however, sensing her despair I feel it is more important to be there with her. I say to Linda, "I'll be right there," and hang up the phone.

As I walk past Clair's cubicle, knowing I can no longer reassure my co-workers, I tear up and say, "Linda says my two children were in the fire. I'm going home." Clair's hand goes up to her mouth. I quickly walk off. This is no time for chitchat. The need to get home overrides everything else! I open the lab's front door and walk out to the van.

Just as I'm about to open the van door, Ed comes running out and says, "Do you want me to drive?" I do a quick self-examination; before Ed came out I had been thinking, take it easy, drive safely. I tell him, "I can drive." Ed says, "Shall I go with you?" I am touched by his concern and say, "Sure, come on." He gets in.

Before we are even out of the parking lot I say, "These two children are my angels." I go on to explain that there is an unusually powerful spirit in my youngest girl. You can just feel spiritual brilliance coming out of her when she is held close! I have felt this with all of my kids, but it is extra powerful with these two. That is why I refer to them as my two little angels. As I drive up North Boulevard, I wonder if I really am okay to drive. I suppress the urge to rush, a feeling that is amplified by a world reeling in slow motion around me. I force myself to talk to Ed, hoping to ward off the shock building inside of me. I talk about how Vaughn is an exceptionally bright kid. I wait to turn left onto the Lewisville Highway. The cars are moving in slow motion. After successfully turning onto the highway I sense that Ed is relieved. I'm exercising more self-control than he expected. I remind myself, "Don't speed."

It takes forever to travel the next few miles up the Lewisville Highway. Every minute is torturous. I can see a huge plume of smoke several miles off to my left. I point it out to Ed and say, "That must be it." The column is very black and thick at the top and spreading. Its appearance marks a fire worse than stubble burning in a field. As I finally turn west onto Coltman Road the column of smoke is huge. It shoots high into the sky. I am in the final mile on my way home. I notice that the column is thinning near the bottom. I remark to Ed that they must have it out now.

At the end of that mile I am unprepared for the amount of commotion I encounter. I turn back south for a final 100 yards to my home. There are people everywhere: neighbors, fire engines, cars and a media truck with antennas raised high. I worry I won't be able to get the van close to the house. I don't remember parking. As I run to the house I note that there is nothing but a pile of charred rubble where the truck camper used to sit.

I think to myself as I approach the door, "Maybe they weren't in there. They are somewhere hiding or playing outside. Perhaps Linda found them while I was on my way home."

I walk in the house; it's swarming with people. I see Linda being comforted by friends. The seemingly impenetrable distance between us has finally been reduced to steps. I walk to her amidst a concerned crowd; they part acknowledging my right to approach. Linda cries, and we embrace.

Neighbors and friends try to comfort us. I embrace many of them. Ed is there. I strangely remember thinking to myself that I know I got out of the van with him and walked to the door. I was so overpowered by everything going on around me that I had forgotten Ed was there until he gives me a big bear hug. I try to remember coming in the door with him and can't. I'm having a hard time believing any of this is happening.

Linda relates the events of the morning to me. During the details my hope gives way to despair, then grief, then horror. The part about Aisha's scream is the worst. It hits me between the eyes and has haunted me more than any other detail. The fact that I wasn't there as a father, causes me to feel helpless. I had been away and could not hear or respond to her cry for help. It is as if I can hear her cry, calling to me for help as Linda tells her story. I can hardly stand up but find strength to continue listening.

Aisha went wherever Vaughn went, so Vaughn was in there too. I wish with all my heart that time could go in reverse and we could start the day over. It is just such a short time that has passed. Why? The helplessness is unbearable. This is too sudden, too out of our control, too final!

Linda continues to relate her story to me, how she felt so alone and helpless. My heart sinks again. If only I had stayed home today. I admit to Linda that I would have gone inside the burning camper. Linda remarks that it is a good thing then that I went to work because I would have been seriously injured. I can't help wishing I had been there. If only and again and again, if only.

My emotions become so intense, they are affecting me physically. My head is swimming and my chest hurts. It feels as if my arms and legs are paralyzed. They won't function to grab time and reverse it. I feel like I'm having a childhood nightmare where I can't walk or move. I am powerless to reverse what has occurred no matter how much I will it, no matter how recent the event. The small amount of time that has passed since I last saw my kids is as a small windowpane between us. If I could just shatter it, reach through, grab and save them. Why can't I get them? It only happened a moment ago.

I think, "What about Vaughn? There was no sound from him! What if he started the fire, got out, and is hiding outside somewhere, knowing he was not allowed to play with matches?" I recall a conversation with him when I told him never to play with matches. He had been so curious to watch me start the fire in the fireplace that it worried me. Linda is sure he went in the camper, simply because Aisha wouldn't have gone in alone. I have to be sure. This is killing me.

I go outside and quickly walk past the fire engine to the yellow and black barrier tape set up by the fire department. Lifting the tape, I go under and walk directly toward the charred rubble where my father's camper once stood. I take a searching look. As one of the firemen approach, I say to him, "I'm the father." I look into the rubble but see nothing. Grabbing me in a big bear hug and turning my gaze away from the rubble, the fireman says, "You don't want to look at that, you want to remember them the way they were." I break down, grab him hard and cry. The word "they" gets to me. I now know they are both gone. After a moment he asks me to go and sit on the back of the fire engine, saying they will be over in a few minutes to talk to me.

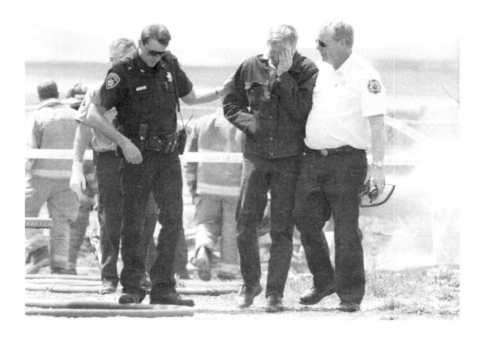

I lift the tape, walk over to the fire engine and sit on the back step. Water has pooled between the raised chrome pattern. I only notice it as it soaks into my pants. It startles me, as if to awaken me from a nightmare. Sadly, after being startled, the nightmare does not go away. I cry for a moment there, waiting for the firemen to come over. I look at the firemen going about their business. I am wet, miserable, and feel exposed to prying eyes. I know the media is close and don't want to be in their story. I think, "This is crazy. I'll wait in the house."

My neighbor, Tim Jephson, stops me, on my way to the house and we embrace. I sit on the back deck, and Tim relates that he has felt a special spirit here. He knows that however painful this is, our kids were meant to go. It is their time, and they are where they need to be. He mentions that others there at our home feel the same thing. Somehow I know this is true but can't help resenting it. It is my kids that are gone! I walk back into the house.

My parents show up. I know this will be very hard on them. Linda had asked my Dad just last week what could be done with the old camper. Dad gives me a hug. Mom gives me a hug. I sense they are uncomfortable with all the people around us. They want to comfort us but are powerless. Mom and Dad lost a son, my brother Devon, and know the clock runs only forward. They are crying.

I am amazed at how fast the news of our tragedy spreads. So many neighbors come to comfort us. I thank them for their concern. We moved into the Coltman community six years ago. Coltman is a small, tight-knit community where everyone knows everyone. I feel that even though the neighbors know us, they didn't know Vaughn and Aisha. Thinking to myself, "How can I help them to know and understand our two angels?" I relate Aisha's "cute-cute" story from that morning. I relate how Vaughn memorized Dr. Seuss' whole ABC book word for word.

Big M little m
Many mumbling mice,
are making midnight music
in the moonlight. . .
mighty nice

Vaughn's face would light up. How I laughed! He really could hear and see those mumbling mice. M was his favorite. The kids had put him up to it to trick Dad into believing that Vaughn could read. How clever they all were.

Vaughn was asleep when I went to work. My last thought of Vaughn before work that morning was, "Don't wake him by saying goodbye." I was about to peek in on him anyway, but dismissed the thought and left. How I wish I had said goodbye.

One of the firemen comes in and asks if there is anything they can do to help notify people. That brings to mind our four older kids. I imagine them blissfully unaware of the terrors at home. I deeply wish to withhold this tragedy from them. I want to spare them this pain and again wish the morning's events could be reversed before my children arrive. I feel for the first time that the reality of the present situation has become real, uncontained and spreading. I can't right it. It is beyond my power. In a subdued voice I say, "We need to tell the kids."

Chapter 4
Breaking the News

Linda

The fire department downtown received my 911-phone call at 1:38 p.m. It was already after 2:00 p.m. when we realized grade school children would be boarding the buses in less than 15 minutes. I called Fairview Elementary and informed the secretary, Janie, of the news. I asked her to keep Sarah, Roslyn, and Isaac from getting on the bus. We did not want them coming home to a scene like this. A friend and neighbor, Eileen, drove to Fairview and picked up our kids. Our oldest child, Dan, was at Rocky Mountain Middle School. I called my best friend, Maryia, at her place of work, told her the news and asked if she would go get Dan. David and I pulled up in front of Dale and Maryia Roberts' home just as Dan was getting out of Maryia's car.

David

Dan's eyes were red. It was evident he knew what had happened. We walked into the game room on the west side of the house and found Sarah, Roslyn and Isaac, playing around the pool table. Sarah was happy and smiled as we entered. It was clear she had not yet been informed of the tragedy. When Sarah saw us she stopped, sensing the sorrow in our faces. Isaac and Roslyn in unison instinctively looked up and quieted.

We sat down on a large, corner-sectional couch in the Roberts' game room. Our Bishop, David Keck, the Relief

Society President, JoAn Nicols and her second counselor, Cathy McBride, were all with us. I stood up and was about to talk when Linda said, "There has been a fire. Vaughn and Aisha were in it, and they're dead." It was just like Linda, to be very short and concise; no mincing her words, similar to how she informed me earlier. I soon found out this came from having to convince other people of the news. Linda had lost patience with bringing people gradually through shock and on to acceptance.

My dad owned two campers. One is stored at the side of his house in Idaho Falls and the other was the one that burned on our property in Coltman. Initially, upon hearing the news, they ran outside their own home thinking that Linda was telling them the camper next to their home was on fire. When they did get back to the phone, it was difficult to convince them that two grandchildren had died in their camper stored on our property.

When something like this happens, frustration can win over patience. Linda reacted with frustration towards my parents. It was my Dad's camper. She had asked him to move it. My parent's pain intensified, sensing the aggravation and lack of patience Linda had for them. When pain runs this deep, it is anyone's guess how people will act and react.

My reaction was disbelief at the events unfolding around me. I looked on through cried out eyes, still wanting to cry. Strangely my thoughts and focus seemed far removed from what I was seeing and sensing, as if I were viewing the world through a tube from a distance. Seeing Sarah, Isaac, and Roslyn break into a heart-wrenching cry was too much. We can sense when our children cry with real sorrow. Again the tears broke through from some as yet hidden reserve. Dan, seeing his family cry, again joined in.

What comfort could be given? Nothing stops pain! It ripped through each of us and tore us apart inside. We cried. We hugged as if grasping each other could fight off the growing rip in our hearts. Somehow it did bring some relief. Slowly, we began to talk through crying. Slowly we conversed and related sad details to our children. Details were salt in the wound. We began our walk together in pain.

Linda and I went out behind Robert's home and walked along a wooden horse fence, just the two of us. We needed quiet. We shared a few moments of solitude. Maryia walked out and gently pulled us back on course. A few family members had shown up.

My brother Reed was out front. We hugged. Reed related his sorrow and wished for those times when cousins were to play together. I could only reach deep and tell the story of two angels who came to visit us. They must have been too pure, too great to remain with us. How I will miss them! I cried.

My sister Anita showed up. Why is it that the pain is greater when meeting family? Dad, Mom, Reed and Anita were each greeted with difficulty. It is hardest to share bad news with the ones who are closest to us. I love them all deeply. I cried with each of them.

About an hour had passed. We had informed our children and inevitably needed to face the responsibilities that awaited us at our house. Upon arriving home we went inside and were greeted by even more people. We embraced, drawing a little strength from each person. Thank you for being there.

Chapter 5
Grandma's Heartache

Linda

It was disconcerting to learn that while we were at Dale and Maryia's house, my mother had been taken to the hospital. My friend, Faith, noticed my mother's physical distress. Faith said, "Something kept making me look at your mom. At first I thought she was overcome by emotion, but as I kept looking I noticed she was more in physical distress than emotional. Several times I asked, 'Are you okay?' and she would say, 'I'm fine.' She didn't look okay. She kept putting her hand on her heart. I went outside and said to one of the ambulance guys, 'There's a lady in there and she's in trouble' . . ."

Before I called Mom with the news, she had been trying to mow her lawn. She had successfully pulled the cord and started the mower but when she tried to push, sharp pains would shoot up her neck. She gave up trying to mow the lawn, and for a few more minutes was down on her knees weeding a flowerbed until the phone rang. If my mom had been mowing the lawn when I called she would not have heard the phone. My mother was the first person I called. I needed her.

The paramedics tried to get Mother to ride in the ambulance. Mom refused service, insisting that her daughter Catherine from Pocatello would be there soon to take her.

May 11, 1999 Catherine's perspective (Linda's sister)

Catherine

I had talked to Mom on the phone a long time that morning, at least an hour. After hanging up the phone my goal was to weed the front flowerbed. Before I weeded my two little boys and I needed lunch. I had just sat down to eat when the phone rang. I looked at the caller ID and read DAVID JAMISON. I was in a cheerful mood and thought, "Oh that's my sister, wanting to tell me more about her creative project ideas."

When a man's voice identified himself as a member of the Idaho Falls Fire Department, my mood instantly changed. "Is this Catherine?" he inquired. I became alarmed. My heart was pounding, as I thought, "Oh No! – It's Mom's heart, something happened to my Mom." "Yes! This is her," I answered.

"There has been a tragedy in your family. Are you alone?" he asked. "No, my two little boys are here with me. What is wrong? What has happened?" I frantically asked. The fireman then said, "I need you to sit down." I was quickly losing patience with the fireman's slow approach. Again I repeated, "What is wrong?"

I then received an answer beyond my wildest nightmare, "There has been a fire, in a camper. Your sister's two youngest children . . ." "OH NO!!! Is my sister okay? Is she burned?" "She's okay, but the children are dead." I then asked for Linda but was told she was not there at the house. Mother got on the line instead. We were both crying too hard to understand each other. I repeatedly assured Mom that I was coming. I was leaving right now.

The fireman came back on line and said, "I don't want you to drive, is there anyone you can call?" I answered, "Yes, my husband Mark." Again I was cautioned, "Promise me you won't get in your car and drive."

I immediately called Mark at Wall-to-Wall Carpet. Lois answered the phone. From the tone of my voice she knew it was an emergency and said to my husband, "Mark, you've got to take this call now!" Mark only heard FIRE, TRAILER, and DEAD, and then literally hung up on me. Mark thought it was our kids in the trailer we own, that is parked next to our driveway.

As I waited for Mark's arrival my mind had a hard time accepting the news. My thoughts were rampant: "This doesn't happen to people I know, especially my sister. . . this can't happen. . . Vaughn and Aisha are my kids' closest cousins. . . they're playmates! . . When Linda and I were pregnant with Aisha and Bradley we laid on the waterbed and laughed because we couldn't get off. . ."

Shortly after Mark arrived, a friend who lives farther down our street stopped by. Jill didn't have a reason to stop, just that she felt prompted by the Spirit. "Cathy, I'll take care of your kids. Just go!" she commanded.

All the way to Idaho Falls Mark was going as fast as our little Mercury Sable would go, at least 90 mph. I said to Mark, "Can't you go any faster?" His reply, "I can't go any faster!" Luckily there were no cops out that afternoon.

Somewhere along I-15, I experienced a flashback. I saw Linda and I at Darby Girls Camp, sitting around a fire, talking amongst a group of girls. The fire brought warmth and comfort. Somehow that setting was a stark contrast to the unbelievable events of today.

As we got to the Lewisville Highway with eight miles more to go, my mind turned to denial, "What am I going to tell everyone when this isn't all true?" Then we turned west onto Coltman Road and the sight of black smoke slapped me back to reality. People were everywhere. After letting me out in front of Linda's house, Mark had to drive way up the road to find a parking spot.

A dark blue Wood Funeral Home van was backed up in the driveway. Immediately I ran back to where the camper once stood. I was shocked to see nothing but the soaked, still smoldering pile of charred nothingness. I let my presence be known, "I'm Linda's sister! Those children are my niece and nephew."

Having been turned away from the scene, I then ran to the front of the house and up the ramp to the open front door. "Linda, Linda!" I yelled as I came inside. I was confused at all the people, "Where did they come from?" A young boy, sitting on the leather couch, was being questioned by a police officer. A nice looking man approached me and said, "I'm David Keck, I'm David and Linda's Bishop." Faith then came to me and said, "Your sister has gone to Maryia's house."

Next my eye caught Mother sitting on a couch in the next room. She had her hand to her mouth and was crying. I ran to Mom and fell into her arms. We held each other and wept.

Faith again approached me, this time putting her arm around my waist as she reminded me of the seriousness of my mother's condition, "Your mother is not well. You've got to focus on her now; she's got to get to the hospital." At this same moment, one of the paramedics was talking to Mark, "You've got to get your mother-in-law to the hospital now." Mark and I each took Mom by an arm as we escorted her out of the house and into our car.

Mom insisted on stopping at her house before going onto the hospital so she could change her clothes. While Mother was changing I wrote Dad a note that said, "Call Catherine's cell," and taped it to the hanging light over their kitchen table so Dad wouldn't miss it. My brother Terry came in before we left, and I told him the news. We went on to the EIRMC (Eastern Idaho Regional Medical Center), and Terry waited for Dad.

Dad was up in Rexburg car shopping. When Dad drove onto the driveway Terry was waiting at the side gate. Before Dad could get out of the car Terry was waving him down and at the car door motioning for Dad to roll down the window. "What on earth is going on Terry?" asked my dad. Terry only told Dad that, "Vaughn and Aisha are dead, and Mother's in the hospital." Dad immediately guessed that Linda had been in an automobile accident. Dad went into the house and called me. I didn't give him any more details. I simply said, "Come to the hospital, Dad. Come now!"

After a few minutes of watching the Emergency Room staff work on mother (her heart was in fibrillation), I went back out to the lobby area where I silently began to pray, "Please Dear Lord, you can't take all three – you can't take my mom!" In a few more minutes Dad walked through the big double glass sliding doors; we remained standing in the ER lobby as I broke the news. When we went into Mom's E.R. room, Dad sat down on a chair. I became quiet as I watched the sad information take hold of his mind. Color drained from his cheeks as he leaned forward, placing face in hands and elbows on knees.

Mom was admitted overnight. As soon as she was situated in her room, Mark left for Pocatello to be with our kids. Dad was terribly concerned for Linda. We said goodbye to Mom and drove out to Linda's house. When we got there we were told that David and Linda had returned from Maryia's house but were now on their way to the hospital to see Mom. The crowd had gone. Only David's family members remained in the house-Delmar, Rosalie, Reed and Brenda (David's brother and wife), Anita (David's sister) and her three kids, Aarica, Brad and Becky. In heavy silence we all sat down and waited.

I returned to EIRMC later that evening, and together Mother and I endured the longest and saddest night of our lives. Mom kept begging the nurses and doctor to be released: "My daughter needs me; I need to be with my daughter." Their response was always, "We've got to get your heart under control."

The next day a lady came to our room and shared a dream she had the previous night. The woman said, "I am not of your LDS faith, but I am a very religious woman. I had a dream last night. I was told that an angel came and took your grandchildren very quickly; they suffered no pain."

Linda

I was grateful for this woman's dream. It confirmed what I already believed and hoped was true, that

Vaughn's and Aisha's spirits were separated from their bodies before they suffered any physical pain. I am also thankful for Faith's awareness of my mother's condition when the rest of us were too distracted to notice.

Faith was equally observant of Vaughn and Aisha's other Grandma, Rosalie Jamison. While out on the front lawn she looked at Rosalie and said, "You look like you need a hug," then embraced my mother-in-law. To this day Rosalie tears up when she tells me of the incident. She refers to Faith as an angel.

Chapter 6
The Grief Puzzle

During that first sleepless night as David and I lay awake crying and talking, we remembered the September evening three and a-half years previous to the fire when our son Isaac suffered a near drowning, at the Green Canyon natural hot spring swimming pool northeast of Rexburg. The reason we experienced Isaac's near death came with power and clarity.

Grieving is like putting together a 10,000-piece puzzle. Remembering Green Canyon was like opening our puzzle box for the first time and discovering a very large segment had come from the factory already assembled. After taking the near drowning section out, we continued to stir around the puzzle pieces and discovered other significant memories. By dawn's first light we realized these Life Experience sections were a huge blessing. These recollections, combined with our knowledge of the gospel of Jesus Christ, were like having a grief puzzle with fully interlocking edges. Already we were beginning to see the big picture and knew our lives were not going to fall apart.

My Green Canyon Experience
Teaches Me Not to Blame.

David

On Friday **September 29, 1995**, I was invited to go to Green Canyon with the scouts as the swimming merit badge counselor. I had been released as the assistant scoutmaster the previous Sunday. My kids wanted to go along, which scout policy doesn't allow; so rather than not go at all we drove up as a family in our own vehicle.

My family was in the pool having fun when the scouts began to arrive. I remember playing with my three year old boy, Isaac, on my shoulders. I played until I was worn out. I took him off my shoulders, placed him onto the pool's cement deck then sank down into the water, resting my back against the wall.

In a moment Linda called loudly from across the pool, "David, where is Isaac?" He was out of the water behind me where I had placed him, or so I thought. I stood up and looked around. I did not see him anywhere. "He must have walked around to the hot pool," I suggested. As Linda got out of the main pool and looked into the adjacent hot pool room I thought to myself, "Don't worry; he's here."

I stood up, carefully scanned the pool and did not see him. I walked a wide circle in the shallow end, slowly looking for him. Linda came back, walked down the steps, into the water and back over to her previous spot where she settled down into the water. As I got to the wall, I looked at Linda expectantly, wondering, "Had she found him or not?"

Linda's back suddenly straightened up like a rod as she popped back up out of the water and yelled, "David, where is Isaac?"

With this my efforts took on more urgency. "Search the pool first then the restrooms," I thought. Linda walked diagonally across the pool to the area just below where I had been looking; I continued my course around the shallow end.

As I got to the center of the pool I heard a terrified scream from my wife. I looked around and saw her pull Isaac out of the water about 15 feet farther toward the deep end than I had just been. She lifted him up above her shoulder with one hand in his belly; Isaac folded over her hand. His little face was purple. I was startled and immediately rushed through the water toward my wife as she continued to scream, "Help!"

Linda pushed Isaac's limp body up onto the side of the pool by the chain link fence. A young lifeguard turned Isaac face down and had just given him a compression as I arrived. I remember thinking to myself, "That's not good enough," as I jumped out of the water and took over. I turned Isaac onto his back and gave him two more compressions just above his belly and below the diaphragm; a lot more water came out this time. Placing my fingers against his neck, I felt for a pulse but found none. I then placed my ear against his chest and listened. There was a pulse! I gave him mouth to mouth and filled his lungs with air. I vaguely remember hearing someone giving instructions. The voice sounded distant.

As I intently focused on Isaac, the outside world faded away. It was as if Isaac and I were alone in a luminous white bubble. I could hear and see only my boy.

Isaac threw up. A male voice penetrated the bubble and said, "Clear his mouth." I turned my son on his side and cleared his mouth. I compressed him again to help clear the air from the first breath and make room for more. The air gurgled out, blowing more water out. I gave him another breath. His face was pinking up. He threw up some more.

Again I became conscious of someone in the pool, talking to me. The voice said, "Turn him on his side and clear his throat." I turned him and swiped my finger two to three times, deep into his mouth, clearing his mouth and airway. There was a lot of vomit, and I didn't want to blow it deep into his lungs.

I was about to give another breath when, to my great relief, he breathed in on his own. I waited for the next breath, but it didn't come.

The bubble began to shrink around us. We were in a luminous isolated place that limited my focus and attention to the area immediately around Isaac's face. Hoping to clear more water out of his lungs, I compressed Isaac again; this time very little water came out. With another breath, Isaac's face pinked up and showed signs of life. I gave him several additional breaths then assisted his exhale with light compressions just below the diaphragm.

Isaac finally started breathing on his own. I felt an incredible sense of relief. He made a moaning sound as I watched him breathe. The private bubble we were in began to clear. The feeling was like looking through a video camera as it zooms back out. The outside world came rushing in. I knew Isaac would be okay.

I looked up, to my right, through the chain link fence, which separated the pool from the main entrance, and noticed the scout troop. They looked back, entranced by what they were seeing. I remember being puzzled at how I hadn't noticed them sooner. My puzzlement grew as I looked down to my left and saw people formed into a crescent below me in the water, all with very worried expressions on their faces. I could have reached out and touched them but hadn't noticed them until that moment. I looked up slightly and saw Linda, farther back in a second larger crescent of people.

I said to her, "Go get the kids out and ready to go home." Some of the people became even more shocked at this point when they discovered the boy's father performed the resuscitation.

I picked Isaac up, carried him into the men's room and laid him down by my feet on a towel. Isaac was resting his head on his hands and crying, obviously not feeling well. A friend of mine, Grover Wray, (we had been in Sweden together as missionaries) happened to be there and had witnessed the resuscitation. Grover came into the men's room and asked if I needed any help in giving him a blessing. I had been thinking about a blessing but didn't know whom to ask. We went off into another room and blessed Isaac. (Almost two years later on August 23, 1997, Grover and his wife Sue lost their four-year-old son Kody Louis Wray in an automobile accident.)

It's strange but from the instant I saw Linda pluck Isaac up and out of the water with a purple face, I knew everything was going to be okay. During the resuscitation this feeling comforted me, and remained with me during his blessing and throughout the rest of the evening. I took Isaac into the small restroom and finished getting him ready for the trip home. He was alert and crying softly.

We were about to leave when the ambulance came. I was surprised to see them there. The pool owners were required to call them. The paramedics examined Isaac and said there would be no ambulance fee if he rode back in our own vehicle. We decided to have him ride with us. One of the young ladies with the paramedic crew volunteered to ride with us to keep an eye on Isaac. That was very kind. We focused on his ability to stay alert and awake. This was a way to monitor any brain trauma. He seemed alert and okay; there were no symptoms of brain trauma. We stopped at Madison Memorial Hospital in Rexburg. It still felt like we were a long way from home.

Then, to our surprise, we discovered that Dr. Anderson, an old acquaintance who also works at the Eastern Idaho Regional Medical Center (EIRMC) in Idaho Falls, was on duty. His presence there was a great comfort to us. He took an x-ray of Isaac's lungs. A feathery whiteness indicated the presence of fine water droplets. Dr. Anderson said the most dangerous thing facing us now was the possible onset of pneumonia as a result of the many forms of bacteria inhabiting hot pool water. He wanted to keep Isaac overnight for observation. We asked if we could take Isaac on to EIRMC instead. Dr Anderson agreed on the condition that we take him there nonstop. They called ahead and informed EIRMC of his condition as we loaded Isaac up.

The drive to Idaho Falls was quiet. The EMT that rode with us from Green Canyon was gone. With this privacy I opened up. I began to reflect back on the events of the evening. I broke down and started to cry as I visualized the way I had witnessed Linda stand up and walk straight across the pool to the spot where she plucked Isaac out of the water.

I thought to myself, "Here my child is drowning, and I am so oblivious, and even annoyed at Linda's request to locate him."

The Spirit was strong in the van at that moment. My pride was gone. I felt ashamed for having been annoyed with her in the pool. I knew I was no spiritual giant. I knew Linda had been in tune enough with the Spirit to save Isaac. Had she not been, Isaac would have died in a short few minutes underwater.

At that moment I came to trust what some call 'women's intuition' or in my case, I came to believe in Linda's ability to hear and feel the Spirit. It was as if the Spirit was talking to me and letting me know this. I wondered why the Spirit had been so quiet while Isaac was drowning. I felt confused over this and hurt that I had been oblivious to the suffering of my child drowning only 20 feet away from me.

When we arrived at EIRMC in Idaho Falls Isaac was checked and admitted into the hospital over night. They monitored his blood oxygen level and gave him an IV bag with antibiotics. He stayed in the hospital 24 hours. By Saturday evening Isaac looked much better although he still felt a little sick to his stomach. Linda was very worried about him but the doctor was convinced that everything would be fine and decided to allow him to go home.

Isaac was sitting in a wheelchair ready to be wheeled out to our van. I was happy! Just about then Isaac threw up all over the floor. Linda remained worried and uncomfortable about taking Isaac home. She tried to convince the doctor he should stay longer. He reassured her that the upset stomach was a normal side effect of some of the medications he'd been given. We were informed of things to monitor during Isaac's recovery. Other than Isaac being very lethargic for about one week, he did fine.

Three and one half years later, the confusion I felt at the time this incident occurred became clear. I now understood why I needed to learn some very important lessons that evening coming home from Green Canyon. It was simple. I was not to doubt that if the Lord wanted to intervene to save one of my children, he could. Linda was capable of picking up the warning and acting on it. Even if I were standing right there, I might be oblivious to these promptings. I know that Linda can and does receive promptings for the welfare of our children. I can't deny this. I had witnessed a powerful intervention as it unfolded before my eyes.

There was no intervention for Vaughn and Aisha; they were allowed to go. I don't understand the reasons, but I trust someday I will gain a better understanding and come to terms with their loss. Until that day, I have to live in faith. I believe that my Green Canyon experience taught me to trust Linda and helped prepare me for the loss of Vaughn and Aisha. There is no doubt, that had I not had this earlier humbling experience, I personally would have struggled. I felt responsible and guilty for several weeks after Isaac's near drowning. Linda continued selflessly to love me through this entire experience, without blaming me. How could I possibly now blame her?

The Spirit Prompts

Linda

I am extremely grateful for the promptings of the Holy Ghost to save Isaac. I believe Isaac was on the verge of death considering how much time I had wasted while checking the hot pool room. When I got back to the spot where Roslyn was waiting, I then started moving through the water in a diagonal direction. I did not know where Isaac was nor could he be seen until I was within three feet. I know the Spirit guided me. Had I gone in any other direction I would not have found my son in time.

I am also thankful for the Spirit prompting my former Ricks College roommate Brenda Bassett (Moseley now) for calling me earlier that morning. I hadn't talked to Brenda for over fifteen years. We must have talked for at least a half hour. Her unexpected long distance call changed my mood for the better. Before her call I had made up my mind not to go swimming. After visiting with Brenda, I was suddenly very enthused about swimming and began packing the suits and towels.

I called Sheila to see if her oldest daughter, Heather could baby-sit. I wanted to have fun and did not want a baby in my arms. Vaughn was 16 months old. (I was two months pregnant with Aisha.) Sheila later told me that when I came through their front door and stood waiting for Heather, an impression came to her that something was going to happen at Green Canyon that night. "They won't have baby Vaughn, so everything will be okay." Sheila's intuition was accurate in every detail.

Had I been holding toddler Vaughn in my arms I would not have had the freedom to act as I was guided. When I got to Isaac he was completely blue and totally unconscious, hanging like a jellyfish, feet, hands and head down. His back was rounded and closest to the surface. I grabbed Isaac and carried him about four feet to the pool's edge. After lifting him up onto the cement deck, I stayed in the pool and screamed, "HELP!" three more times. Grover Wray later said that my first scream silenced the pool.

I was afraid and found myself backing away from the scene. I held Roslyn close. Two women came and stood with me; one held my hand. Both of them would tell me things like, "He's breathing now. He's going to be okay." I would watch for a few seconds, then look away, then watch, look away. I felt weak.

I remember the scouts gathering along the outside of the chain link fence, gawking, some of them with mouths wide open. Later I was told one of the scouts said that to witness Isaac's near drowning was a spiritual experience. David resented that statement. It had been too painful for him to see it that way.

Early Saturday morning September 30, while in the hospital Isaac said two things I will never forget. First he asked me if he had been born again. And a short while later he announced that, "Jesus saved me." This statement combined with the memory of what Isaac looked like when pulled from the water, plus the luminous bubble surrounding my husband and son that David talked about, causes me to wonder how near death Isaac really was. I am grateful for Jesus Christ.

Chapter 7
Sad Duties

Having spent the whole of Tuesday night connecting our Green Canyon experience and other puzzle pieces, David and I were in a state of exhaustion as we set out Wednesday morning to accomplish the sad duties of funeral arrangements. Catherine and my dad came with us to Wood Funeral Home. The man helping us was very patient. Twice I fell asleep and once Dad broke into a sob.

On Thursday David and I went to the Teton Mall to buy Vaughn's burial clothes. We found a little vested suit with a graphic design embroidered on the white collar that reminded us of the k-nex building pieces our little boy so loved to play with.

After purchasing the clothes we walked out of JC Penny's to the center court where we ran into Mrs. Barrie's fifth grade class. They were on a fire safety field trip. (Sarah later told me that one of the demonstrations was showing kids how to escape out of a burning trailer. I wondered if that decision to teach fire survival skills was made because of the Jamison tragedy two days previous?)

As I was showing Sarah the funeral clothes I became aware that some of her classmates were watching me. I did not pull Vaughn's suit out of the shopping bag, but simply opened it wide enough for her to see. I thought it an odd coincidence that we would run into Sarah's class while they were on a fire safety field trip. I became self-conscious and wondered if there was any significance to the timing of this center court mall scene. There I was, holding the evidence of what can happen when kids play with matches.

During the three days between the fire and funeral while David and I were away from our home making sullen decisions, our house was taken over by friends or the "army of women," as my dad refers to them. They performed all manner of household chores; collected the dozens of cards, food and gifts thoughtful people brought, and one friend in particular kept the press away, for which I am thankful.

Our front room became a florist shop. I have never seen such an outpouring of care and concern. We felt loved.

Chapter 8
The Funeral

On the way to the church Saturday morning, for the first time since before the fire, I noticed the sky was no longer blue. White clouds had stopped moving on to Wyoming. They were gathered in massive layers, crowded and bunched up behind each other. Dark and heavy with grief, they looked as if they had come to attend our children's funeral.

Several people told me later that watching two child-sized caskets being pushed into the chapel and up the aisle was overwhelmingly sad. The sight of our thirteen-year-old son Daniel pushing Vaughn's coffin was heart wrenching. People wept.

The funeral was extremely well attended. David and I were so grateful for the support and love. I had dozens of friends come, some from 20 years ago. Friends of my parents, who didn't even know me, came. After the funeral, many of these people were generous in their compliments toward David's talk and mine. Their comments buoyed us up . . . "That was the best funeral I've ever been to," or "The spirit was so strong." I agree that Heavenly Father blessed us with an out-pouring of the Spirit.

We recorded our funeral talks. Following the "Our Last Morning Together" part of my talk I said, "I believe the Lord prepared me for my children's deaths, through three meaningful experiences which have occurred during my married life." These three events along with the Green

Canyon memory are all sections of our grief puzzle. Recognizing them early helped tremendously in coping with the tragedy.

First, in September of 1986, David discontinued his schooling at the U of I in Moscow. We moved to Rexburg, Idaho, where he enrolled at Ricks College. We found a basement apartment in a neighborhood that was in the Rexburg 15th Ward. Ronald K. Messer, my former Ricks College English 101 professor, was the Bishop.

I was asked to help in the church nursery. This is where I met and got to know little blonde headed Kami. Sid and Karen are her parents. David and Sid were home teaching partners. During the day of December 2, 1986, little four-year-old Kami was killed in an automobile accident. I heard the news later that evening at the ward Relief Society Christmas Party. I attended the funeral. When I shook Sid's hand he was very strong. He was not crying, though Karen, his wife was a little bit. An impression came over me that said, "Pay attention; you are going to need his example someday." My journal entry of December 9, 1986, tells about Kami's death. The last sentence reads, "Karen and Sid held up well at the funeral, especially Sid."

Second, I had a dream. Very short and simple but the kind that awakens you with the knowledge that something really bad is going to happen. In the dream, I was sitting on the long brown footstool I had made in high school. I was crying or rather sobbing, like I had never done in my entire life. Maryia, my best friend, was sitting next to me on the bench. She had one arm around my shoulder, comforting me.

The third and most recent experience was a conversation I had in November 1998, at the LDS Church Cannery with Linda Robertson. Linda is the mother of Marcia Parrish, who lives in our Coltman 2nd Ward. Linda and Dayle Robertson had come from Oregon to spend Thanksgiving with the Parrish Family.

On the last Friday of November I was scheduled to help can chicken chunks at the cannery. I did not want to go that morning, but decided to anyway. I was late, which turned out to be a blessing because Linda Robertson was also late. Instead of having to wear those big plastic aprons, hair nets, gloves and oversized rubber boots while standing at the noisy conveyor belts cutting up chicken, we got to stay in the box room where it is quiet enough to talk.

A cannery shift lasts three to four hours. She and I talked nearly the entire time. The conversation was personal and spiritual. Linda had given birth to seven children and three of those kids have died in car wrecks. The first child to die was their 18 year-old son, Lindsey. About two weeks before Lindsey died Linda had a dream of an imminent death in her family. She was asked to decide who was going to die, her husband or her oldest son. In her dream she pondered and eventually determined she could not support seven children without her husband, so it would be Lindsey who would have to go. Before her dream ended, she had worked out all the plans for his funeral and upon awakening, dismissed the whole idea. Two weeks later Lindsey died in a car wreck and the plan was put into action.

During Linda's telling of her dream I was absolutely riveted on every word she spoke. Six years later, as I write these words, the thought I was having is still vivid and clear: "I absolutely agree; I would rather have a child pass on instead of my husband."

That is when I gave my answer. God the Father knows our thoughts. I did not audibly have to say the words. (Ten years later in December 1990, the Robertson's lost two daughters in a car wreck; Bekkie age 30 and Rachelle age 25. Bekkie had only been married 4 months. Rachelle was single.) Bekkie, Lindsay and Rachelle are the oldest three of the Robertson's seven children.

I concluded my funeral address by saying....

"I now want to bear my testimony. I am so thankful that I did not lose my testimony while standing on our back deck, watching the camper burn and yelling at the dispatcher. Many people see it as an accident that could and should have been prevented. I believe it was an accident that the Lord allowed to happen and Vaughn and Aisha were meant to go. I am not angry with God. Good will come from the deaths of my children. Good has come already, *and I will see to it that enormous good comes from it the remainder of my life.* I bear you my testimony that God lives, Jesus is the Christ, in the name of Jesus Christ, Amen."

David's Funeral Address:

I feel as if a part of my heart is missing. The emotional attachment we develop with our children, though intangible, is a very real, physical thing. As I lay in bed during the first sleepless night after losing Vaughn and Aisha, I could feel a great emptiness in my heart. I wondered, how can I possibly function, how can I get around this emptiness?

There is no substitute for the loss of two children. Perhaps I could find something and build around this great emptiness. I imagined scaffolds, planks and building materials. I thought, "Perhaps I can somehow bridge over, under, and around this emptiness, thereby avoiding the pain?"

How naive I was.

For just a moment, I felt I wanted to be alone to mourn the loss of my children... Again, how naive I was.

With the first few hugs and the first few tears shed in the company of dear friends, I came to the realization that I am not alone in my suffering, the realization that the emptiness I speak of was not just confined to my own heart.

It resides in the hearts of anyone who knew Vaughn and Aisha.

It resides in the hearts of anyone who loves their own child or children.

It resides in the hearts of anyone sensitive to the pain and suffering of a neighbor, friend or relative.

It became apparent that an attempt for me to build a structure massive enough to enclose all of this emptiness in all of these hearts would be a futile attempt.

Immediately a different and far more natural process began to work on the emptiness within my heart.

This process was reflected by a grandmother, with a troubled heart, lying in the hospital grieving the loss of her two grandchildren, and wishing she could be at the side of her daughter. She too felt the great emptiness in her heart.

As she lay there she recalled again and again that special shopping trip with Aisha and Vaughn. She rehearsed over in her mind every smile, every word, and every action of her grandchildren on that day. She recalled each astute remark of Vaughn. She relived life through the wonder in Aisha at getting her new birthday dress.

Each memory was carefully noted. Each detail was sought out. Then the precious memories were carefully tucked into her heart. No attempt was made to build around the emptiness she felt. Memories were being used to fill in the emptiness.

Others who knew Vaughn and Aisha also came forward with stories.

Sister Johnson: Vaughn would say, "That's right," in class to agree with her lesson points as if he was the authority who could confirm points of truth. She also related that they loved the primary songs, "Popcorn Popping on the Apricot Tree" and "If You Chance to Meet a Frown."

Sister Clayson said, "During a lesson on table manners, Vaughn was very good at directions and would put his hands down to his side between instructions."

Those with any memory of Vaughn and Aisha were sharing them with us. I, too, searched the previous weeks, looking for memories.

I recalled the many sweet hugs and kisses from Aisha, my "Goongula." Her grandparents were jealous because such sweetness was strictly reserved for Mommy and

Daddy. Grandmas and Grandpas are notorious for trying to get at those sweets. Be warned, they may even resort to bribery. I recalled a trip to town with Isaac and Vaughn. I stopped by the Army Surplus Store. I wasn't looking for anything in particular. The main attraction was the wonder I saw in Isaac and Vaughn. In the back of the store Vaughn noticed all the parts. He noticed some tires. Vaughn said to me, "We could build a car with this stuff." He just knew he had stumbled onto the source of the automobile.

In getting information together for Vaughn's and Aisha's life sketches, we got together as family and friends and brainstormed for any memories we could recall.

I took those along with my own and the ones shared by others and placed them into the emptiness within my heart. My heart felt much better.

For Grandma and Grandpa Jamison, who recently returned from a mission in Little Rock, Arkansas, memories have been few. Take these we have shared today and fill the emptiness in your heart.

For anyone who knew Vaughn and Aisha, for anyone who loves their own child or children, for anyone sensitive to the pain and suffering of a neighbor, friend or relative, for anyone here today, take these memories and fill that empty place in your heart with them.

May we all focus on the memories of what we had and not on what we lost? Aisha was capable of great empathy. A frown from Daddy brought immediate attempts to make him happy again. Aisha is here with us. Can we smile for her? She wants us to.

She is not lost, nor is Vaughn.

God knows the beginning from the end. I do not believe that God causes accidents to occur. God can intervene and prevent accidents if He so desires. President Meikle visited us for a few minutes and expressed this same view to us adding that "God only intervenes when it is eternally significant to do so."

I would add that I believe His lack of intervention may also be due to significant factors of an eternal nature.

Linda and I have experienced the intervention of God in saving the life of one of our children. There was no such intervention this time. We believe that it was Vaughn's and Aisha's time to go. As we studied the chain of events that led up to this accident, it became very clear how easily very small interventions could have halted the whole chain of events.

I have a firm belief in the afterlife. Vaughn and Aisha will be missed, but they will not be forgotten. I say these things in the name of Jesus Christ, Amen.

Sheila Gives Vaughn's Life Sketch

Vaughn Joseph Jamison was born June 18, 1994, in Idaho Falls, Idaho, to Linda Gail Smith and David Kay Jamison. He has two brothers and three sisters: Daniel, Isaac, Sarah, Roslyn and Aisha.

Vaughn was the first child born after the Jamison family moved to Coltman. On the morning of June 18, I called Linda to see how she was feeling, and she gave me a Linda answer, "I feel fat and crappy, and I'm having a few labor pains." I said, "Well, do you want to go to a garage sale? There's one just down the road at Andrea Peterson's house." She said, "Why not, maybe it will help get my mind off how rotten I feel." So we headed to the garage sale, and Linda's labor pains started getting harder, and she's making deals on a winter coat and a bike and such when she turns to me and says, "I think we better go." Vaughn was born shortly after.

Vaughn was a baby that had a habit of falling asleep in his high chair at meals, thus making many Kodak moments. The kids remember one time in particular he fell asleep with a big noodle hanging out of his mouth and they said, "Quick, grab the camera."

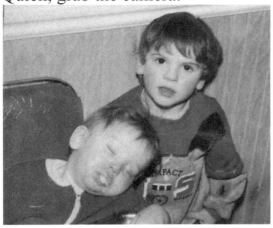

Vaughn had a cry that we called the blat. He would let out a loud, long, monotone cry with his mouth opened so wide his whole face disappeared. One day Vaughn was eyeing Bob McBride's tools, while Bob was working on their house and Bob said, "I don't think that's a very good place for you to play." Vaughn immediately broke into his blat cry, surprising the heck out of Bob.

Vaughn loved anything with wheels! He would be pulling the wagon around the yard and occasionally he would go through a spot that was too narrow for the wagon and get stuck! Dave said he would be madder than a hornet and cry and carry on until they un-stuck the wagon and off he would go again.

Sometimes when Vaughn didn't get his way he would do a dramatic fall to try and get the kids in trouble. Dad caught on to these fake dramatic falls, and one day as Vaughn was doing his act he hit his head and Dave told him, "Now don't you ever do that again."

Vaughn had a daily ritual of picking up Franzle their cat and packing it around. They kept telling him, "If you pick up the cat when he doesn't want to be picked up he'll scratch you!" Vaughn often had a scratch on his face or arms put there by Franzle. I think the cat thought if he scratched, Vaughn would leave him alone. But every time Franzle scratched, Vaughn hit him on the head and eventually the cat learned to quit scratching.

Vaughn loved to bathe and had to have a toy to take in the tub with him. He seldom took a bath alone. Aisha was nearly always in the tub with him.

He loved to play forts and house with Aisha, and you could often find chairs pushed together with a blanket draped over them, entertaining them for hours.

Vaughn loved playing chase with dad. They would run around the island in the kitchen and sometimes Dave would peel off and Vaughn would keep on running around, not realizing Dad wasn't on the other side any more. Sometimes Vaughn would run and hide in the coat closet and David would stand quietly by the front door and wait. The door would open a crack, and Vaughn would squeal and run to the kitchen. He always knew that Dad was waiting on the other side of the door.

Vaughn didn't talk a lot but when he did you couldn't help but be amazed at what he had to say or how he said it. Linda said the cabinetmaker was there to hang the kitchen cabinets, and he was putting holes in the walls where he needed them. Vaughn walked up to him and leaned his body forward and said, "Don't – put – holes – in – our – walls."

He enjoyed picking raspberries at Grandma and Grandpa Smith's and writing on their blackboard. Linda said she was too cheap to buy cold cereal, and so it was a real treat to go to Grandma's and eat bowls and bowls of cheerios.

When Grandpa Smith trimmed his apple trees, Vaughn would drag branches to the pick-up, never tiring of the work. He would help Grandpa stack blocks of wood in a cart to burn as firewood. He loved and enjoyed working.

Vaughn would swing, play Indians with Isaac, or play cars and trucks. One of his Primary teachers said she was amazed at the trucks he could draw. He loved to go to town or to play with friends. The kids would blow bubbles, and Vaughn and Aisha would pop them with delight.

One time his brother Isaac was at the Tortell's, and they loaned him a shirt and a pair of shorts to wear to wrestling. The shorts were returned but not the shirt. It was a red shirt with a dinosaur on the front. They may have wondered what happened to that shirt, but Vaughn wanted to wear it, and it became his favorite. To the Tortell's, thank you!

Vaughn loved church! One teacher commented that he was quiet but easily touched by the Spirit. He was very willing to share with others and was a deep thinker. When you asked him a question he would sit there and think. You could see the wheels turning as he thought, and then he always gave the right answer. Another teacher said, "The first time he sang and did the hand motions in singing time he was so excited. When he smiled his whole face lit up. He was smart and had a good memory. He loved to do skits and role-play in class. One time they were going to the zoo and Vaughn was the dad. He drove the car all over town making all the car sounds: the engine starting, motor rumbling, brakes screeching. He really got into it."

One week in Primary, Vaughn said to his teacher Sister Johnson, "It's cold in here." She said, "Well, the best way I know to get warm is to snuggle." She put Vaughn on one side of her and Jesten on the other side and put her arms around them and they had their lesson. Every week after that, he wanted to sit right next to her. One Sunday while they were waiting for Primary to start he said, "Sin is real bad. Did you know that?" Sometimes when she would be teaching the lesson he would say, "Yes that's right," as if he were the teacher.

During singing time they were going to sing, "If You Chance To Meet a Frown," and Sister Campbell picked someone to turn the frowny face to a smiley face. They started singing, and Sister Johnson looked down and Vaughn was sobbing. She asked him, "What's the matter?" He said, "I wanted to be the happy face." She talked to Carla after Primary and asked her if the next time they sang that song she would let Vaughn be the happy face, and she did. Carla said that whenever they sang that song he would immediately get happy. It was one of his favorite songs.

A few weeks ago Vaughn gave a very special talk in Primary about when he goes on a mission. Nobody knew he would get his mission call so soon. Vaughn started his new mission on May 11, 1999, as he departed mortality in Idaho Falls, Idaho.

There is no doubt in my mind that Vaughn is one of the Lord's valiant. I feel his spirit was mature beyond his four years in age, with qualities of sensitivity to the spirit, deep thinking, good memory, sharing and being a hard worker. He no doubt has yet to fill a great role in our Father's plan.

Children are angels on loan from our Heavenly Father. Some loans are long and some are short, but the price of righteous living can make them ours for eternity.

In closing, I feel Vaughn would have me say to you: If you chance to meet a frown, do not let it stay. Quickly turn it upside down and smile that frown away. No one likes a frowning face; change it for a smile. Make the world a better place by smiling all the while.

Andrea Peterson Gives Aisha's Life Sketch

(Andrea is my other best friend. I thought it appropriate that Andrea give Aisha's life sketch being that I purposely chose to give Aisha an A name after Andrea.)

Aisha Mae Jamison came into the world on the 10th day of May just three short years ago. She filled her place as the sixth and youngest child in a big wonderful family who were ready and waiting for her with open arms and open hearts. Her time upon this earth was brief, yet the impression left upon each who knew her distinctness, her charm, and the rich and tender sweetness of this little child, is indelibly marked upon heart and mind.

Aisha was very particular about whom she would allow to hold her, but everyone loved to be around her! It always seemed sort of magical to me – the way that she would let you in with the look in her warm brown eyes and touch you in such a way that you became very aware that you were indeed in the presence of a very rare, beautiful and deeply intelligent little child.

From her very birth, Aisha forever changed her family. In the words of the poet:

Our birth is but a sleep and a forgetting;
The soul that rises with us, our life's Star,
Hath had elsewhere its setting,
And cometh from afar:
Not in entire forgetfulness,
And not in utter nakedness,
But trailing clouds of glory do we come
From God, who is our home:
Heaven lies about us in our infancy!

(Ode. Intimations of Immortality From Recollections of Early Childhood W. Wordsworth)

This was so true of the infant Aisha. She opened her family's eyes with her innocence; she tickled their minds with her laughter; she filled their hearts to the brim with love and joy and sheer happiness. I witnessed this joy upon her mother's face so many, many times.

It is easy to see why her older sister said that she just wanted to hold Baby Aisha "all by herself," and why all the family shared so willingly and lovingly in Aisha's care, and why every one of them often spoke of the cute little things that Aisha did.

As she grew into toddlerhood, the uniqueness of Aisha became more apparent to those blessed to enter briefly into the world of this little girl. She could entertain herself for very long passages of time with her baby dolls, acting out endlessly the roles of family life. Aisha spent most of her waking hours in the company of her 100% loyal and true blue pal, Vaughn. They shared their forts, their baths, and games of chase and house. A special favorite was the game of "Wolf" that they played with their friends Charlotte and Matthew. Vaughn was Wolf and Aisha and her little friends had a wonderful thrill over and over again screaming and running from Wolf. Aisha loved to be the little traveler – on an errand with her mom, going to Church or visiting the homes of friends Charlotte and Matthew and Abbey. A special visit to sit on the lap of her dear friend, Holly, also pleased Aisha; as did a trip to Millie's room to count pennies when she was in need of special comforting.

It is sometimes said that a girl's best friend is her mother. Aisha and Linda exemplified this bit of wisdom. I remember how Linda could hardly wait for Aisha to be born. She seemed to know she was about to embark on an experience called Wonderful. Aisha loved to push a bucket or a stool over to the kitchen counter to watch Linda cook. She would run as fast as her little legs would carry her, down the stairs to the exciting sound of the washing machine to watch the water pour in. She loved to swing, especially with Mom pushing. And of course, all the countless hours of cuddling and listening to stories, most notably Mother Goose rhymes and Peter Cottontail.

Aisha loved church, especially her nursery class. Never needing prompting, she was perfectly mannered, always saying please and thank you and pushing her chair in at the table. She amazed everyone with her terrific coloring – always in the lines and so carefully done. She was always willing to help with the toys and share them. She had a special love for singing, her bright little face shining as she sang her favorite, "Jesus Wants Me For A Sunbeam." She knew it word for word along with "I Am A Child of God," when she was barely two years old.

Aisha liked to pray at church and at home. On one occasion David went to help her say her prayers before bed, thinking she was ready to learn this, only to witness her do it on her own. She was truly her daddy's little sweetheart. He would ask her, "Are you my Sweetheart?" And she would answer simply "Yes," in that soft little Aisha way.

Aisha thoroughly enjoyed all the pleasures of childhood life, and that is not to exclude that marvelous thing called eating. Aisha loved to eat and ate a lot! To put it into the candid words of her mother, "She was a PORKER!"

Aisha had lots of personal style. She emphatically chose her own outfits, even which pair of PJ's would be suitable for a particular evening. Her favorites were bright colors and florals and all things feminine. At bedtime, she often required a blanket to help her go to sleep. But this was not to be any blanket! It had to be the old baby blanket, which belonged to her older sister, and which was spread so carefully over her sister's bed where she already lie sleeping! When Aisha got out of the bath with her hair all curly and wet, she would run and giggle all the while modestly covering her little self in the cutest Aisha way.

The bliss that was Aisha bubbled over and splashed happily upon all those around her. No greater blessing does life afford us than the love of a little child. Indeed, Aisha helped all of those who knew her to feel in greater measure life's quest: To live our lives well, to love as much as we are able, and to remember to laugh often. She will be greatly missed and often remembered with tenderest affection, the humblest gratitude and the deepest love.

Heaven Weeps
Linda

My friend, Jan, from Utah sang the closing song, "An Early Goodbye." Later Jan told me that just before she started to sing she glanced down at me and saw incredible pain on my face and knew that if she looked again she would not be able to sing. The song was perfect and sung beautifully.

There was a slight drizzle before the funeral. When the south chapel door opened to reveal pallbearers carrying out two, child size caskets the rain increased.

Vaughn's middle name is Joseph, after my father, Grant Joseph Smith. We thought it appropriate that my father dedicate his grandchildren's graves at Grant Central Cemetery.

Watching the burning camper collapse was the most terrifying. But the saddest moment for me was watching my children being laid to rest. This was worse than following their caskets into the chapel. The moment my brother Terry took off his lapel rose and laid it on Vaughn's casket, I saw his tears. My heart began to break. Terry has never married and has no children.

Just as the pallbearers placed the last rose on the caskets, the cumulonimbus clouds released the pile of rain they could no longer restrain. Heaven was literally weeping as we walked away from our children laid to rest in their matching pearl white caskets.

Two Little Angels

Two little angels
Sent from above.
Their voices filled with laughter,
Their hearts filled with love.

A brother and a sister,
Best friends from the start.
Who shared with one another
And touched so many hearts.

Darling little Aisha,
A sweetheart through and through.
A mother's little pride and joy,
Her smile lit up the room.

Silly little "Lady Bug"
Who loved to dance and play.
How we'll miss that little voice,
And the things you used to say.

And little Vaughn, the little man
He could sit for hours,
Drawing cars and trucks for fun,
Or building Lego towers.

Following in Daddy's shadow,
Helping if he could.
Building with the tools like Dad,
That made him feel so good.

So many little things we'll miss.
How precious was the time.
The moments that you spent with us,
We'll treasure in our minds.

We know you're in a special place,
Walking hand in hand,
With Gods own angels round about
To help you understand.

And someday soon we'll meet again,
And forever we will stay.
How happy we will all be then,
On that great and glorious day.

Until then, my precious ones
God keep you safe from harm.
Till eternity calls and once again
We'll hold you in our arms – Forever.

Written 5/14/99
Annette Christiansen

Chapter 9
Summer of '99

On Friday May 14, the day before the funeral a few of my friends had come to our house to help clean and lend emotional support. We were sitting around the kitchen talking, when Sheila announced, "Linda's going to have another baby." I looked at Sheila with curiosity and wondered why this bit of revelation would come to her. In my heart her words rang true.

Within a few weeks I really needed something to help fill the incredible void.

Three weeks after losing Vaughn and Aisha we drove down to Disneyland. I've always felt funny when telling people this. And then I add, "It is a trip we had planned for months. What were we suppose to do, stay home?" Staying home would have been an emotionally damaging choice.

We were at Disneyland three days. Though I felt constantly numb, we had a lot of fun. Our first morning at Disneyland we learned the value of being at the entrance rope early. The first people through could run to any ride and not have to stand in line. Our second morning, we were up, and at the rope before seven o'clock, early enough to be seen, and lucky enough to be chosen, to open Disneyland that day. I've always wanted to thank the lady who let us do that. I think her name was Ginger. Our third morning there, Ginger was not at the rope. I felt bad. I wanted to tell her about Vaughn and Aisha. And how much more memorable Disneyland would be for us because of her kindness. Much to my surprise I saw Ginger and her granddaughter over in the "It's a Small World" Pavilion. (It was Ginger's day off and she was spending it at Disneyland.) I was able to tell her our story and thank her. Ginger does not know the rest of our story. I often think of Ginger and wish I could tell her the rest of our story.

I watched little kids a lot. On the second day I had a thought about Vaughn and Aisha that was particularly comforting… "Mom, we know you are at Disneyland. It's okay; we are glad you are happy. The world we are now in is so much more beautiful that even places like Disneyland don't compare. We are not missing out. Enjoy yourself."

During the late evenings at our hotel my numbness was the worst. I thought about Vaughn and Aisha a lot while watching my four oldest kids play in the pool. And also I began to think about another baby. I remember thinking that June would be a very unhealthy time to conceive. I had not eaten well and had actually lost weight.

After Disneyland we drove down to Fallbrook, California to spend time with David's sister Valerie. After staying with Valerie we drove down to Sea World in San Diego. We arrived about half an hour early. While waiting for Sea World to open I sat in the van and started reading, *The Biography of Gordon B. Hinckley*, written by Sheri L. Dew. In the Preface Sheri talks about her brother's sudden death (heart attack):

"My brother's passing has left an indescribable void. That's the difficult part. But it has also caused me to think deeply about the faith I have embraced my entire life, for during the quiet moments of yearning that follow such experiences you find out what you really believe--and those beliefs either anchor or betray you."

Never has a paragraph of words validated my feelings better. I started to cry. I felt the presence of the Spirit very strong. I knew I had a testimony of Jesus Christ. I was anchored. I am thankful to Valerie for giving us that book.

We returned from vacation just in time for what would have been Vaughn's fifth birthday (June 18th). My brother-in-law wrote the following song and sang it to us at Vaughn's and Aisha's grave for Vaughn's fifth birthday. It is priceless. We all cried.

The Arms of the Lord

Big M little m,
Yes, I'm both your little sweetheart,
Many mumbling mice were making midnight music in the
Moonlight
Now we're walking hand in hand,
As we'll always walk together,
But we're not walking away; we're coming home.
And remember Mom and Dad that we're both doing fine
Cradled in the arms of the Lord.

Chin up brother Dan,
Yes, I know your heart is breaking,
But still you stand tall in their hour of need,
Shine on Sarah Kay; you're a woman in the making,

The time is now to show that you can lead,
And remind our mom and dad that we're both doing fine
Cradled in the arms of the Lord.

Reach out Roslyn,
Cuz we're standing right behind you,
Basking in your beauty and your grace,
Isaac be the man,
There's a spirit to remind you,
That once again we'll stand up face to face,
And remind our mom and dad that we're both doing fine
Cradled in the arms of the Lord.

Big M little m,
Yes I'm both your little sweetheart,
Use these words for comfort when you're down,
Turn your back to the wind,
And your eyes up to the heavens,
Look for us; you know where we'll be found.
And remember one and all that we're both doing fine,
Cradled in the arms of the Lord.

Written by Mark Croft

By the end of July I was not yet with child. In three months I would be turning 39. Maybe this maternity thing was not going to be as easy as it had been six times before.

Maybe a little more faith was needed. On August's Fast Sunday I decided I would fast for 24 hours instead of just skipping breakfast. Even though we were at an Arave

Family Reunion in Chester, Idaho, that first August weekend, I wanted to be home to go to our Sunday church meetings. We specifically prayed for another child.

Three weeks later I took a pregnancy test and discovered David and I had been blessed with the conception of our seventh child. Dr. Hall set the due date at May 1, 2000. Wow, I really was going to have another baby!

Memories Were Not Enough.

David

I would like to focus on the healing process I went through. In the weeks that followed the fire, reflecting upon the happy memories of Vaughn and Aisha was not enough. I missed my kids; I wanted them back.

As I walked toward one of the sheds on the side of my house, I became aware of myself. My shoulders were rolled forward. My feet almost drug as I walked. I felt a darkness lurking in my consciousness. I became intensely aware that the darkness had made surprising gains and meant to grow and overpower me. I felt weak and subdued, out of energy and depressed. I realized that I was making bars that would soon imprison me. I was headed somewhere, that should I venture, there would be no return.

I was slapped back to reality by the seriousness of the position in which I found myself. I realized that I still had choice and could refuse to go into the darkness. I squared my shoulders up and put more spring into my steps. I was amazed at the sudden rush of energy I felt. I realized how easy it is for people to enter into depression. A small dose of apathy and the darkness comes in to stay as a friend. The more familiar and adjusted people become to this new friend, the harder it is to turn him away and refuse entry the next time he pounds on our door.

From that moment on I was determined I would refuse to become depressed. I monitor myself. I have many moments when I cry and ache to hold my children. When I recall the wonderful times I had with Vaughn and Aisha, I see these times as "good sadness." I still cry. I still love. I still see depression there, lurking in the darkness like a beast. I stand against him with optimism, faith, hope and all things good and bright in my life.

People have asked me how I have managed to hold it together. I believe it is through the following realizations:

1. I do not have the power to get through this by myself. I need to reach out for help.
2. I have to refuse to go to the dark place of self-pity.
3. I need to stay busy and get back to work as soon as possible.

I turned to my faith to find the power to cope. I started reading the scriptures and became more familiar with Jesus Christ and His mission. My faith was shaken and put to the test during the aftermath of Vaughn's and Aisha's death. Rather than succumb to doubt, I determined to fight back "the beast" with the comfort and knowledge that were flowing from the scriptures.

We have to reach outward for help. The strength to get through this is not within us. Reach out to family and friends for strength. Reach out to a trusted counselor. I was offered counseling at my work but graciously refused it because of the overwhelming support system I found in family, friends and my faith. As I studied the scriptures, it became very clear that my trusted counselor was my Father in Heaven. I studied the scriptures heavily for several months after Vaughn and Aisha passed. In them I found something that memories alone could not satisfy. In them I found hope. Through them my faith increased. As I read God's counsel in the scriptures, I knew that no "earthly psychology" could compare. I felt healing in my heart. I could not blame God. I felt His love for me as I prayed, and I could not deny His being there.

All my life I have had a testimony of the Gospel of Jesus Christ. I had developed it around many different aspects of scripture. I had built up small bits and pieces here and there. Before the fire I felt secure in my testimony. But when something like this happens, one questions everything and attempts to reestablish his identity. I questioned my beliefs and values. I felt as if a whole context switch was occurring. Most of what I had known in the past now felt insufficient to comfort me. The power and understanding was not within me.

I needed more.

It is as if I were in quicksand, sinking. I needed to stand in an entirely new spot. I needed a whole new perspective. The only thing that saved me was hope in my Savior Jesus Christ. All other tidbits and trinkets of information paled in comparison to a simple need for Him. The sand began to wash away and a sure footing came to view. Jesus Christ became central, illuminating all other beliefs. God, through Christ, is our only hope for resurrection and reunion.

I have a new perspective now. I testify of the healing power of prayer, belief in God the Father, and in His Son, Jesus Christ. I know that anyone who seeks the firm foundation of Jesus Christ, during life's storms, will feel the love of God flow into them, giving them strength to stand.

Chapter 10
No man is an Island

The summer of '99 was busy with my four kids home. When September came and the kids went back to school, I slept; partly because during that first trimester of pregnancy I really was tired, and also to avoid the emotional pain of being alone.

The title of this chapter, no man is an island, is taken from John Donne's famous Meditation XIV, written back in the late 1500's. I first read this piece as a college student at BYU. I was 21 years old. The meaning of this meditation made a big impression on my mind. I underlined my favorite parts and wrote in the margin, "If I ever speak at a funeral--consider this meditation." I did not use it while speaking at my children's funeral, but want to share my favorite underlined parts now, as the theme of this chapter.

All mankind is of one author and is one volume; when one man dies, one chapter is not torn out of the book, but translated into a better language, and every chapter must be so translated. God employs several translators; some pieces are translated by age, some by sickness, some by war, some by justice; but God's hand is in every translation, and his hand shall bind up all our scattered leaves again for that library where every book shall lie open to one another.

No man is an island, entire of itself; every man is a piece of the continent, a part of the main. If a clod be washed away by the sea, Europe is the less, as well as if a promontory were, as well as if a manor of thy friend's or of thine own were. Any man's death diminishes me because I am involved in mankind, and therefore never send to know for whom the bell tolls; it tolls for thee.

As my parents and I read the obituaries, we became saddened on many occasions. 1999 was an unusually bad year; altogether 53 children 19 years old and under passed away in Southeast Idaho. Almost all of the deaths were accidental.

One of these 53 child fatalities happened on February 23, 1999. During the lunch hour that day, a Bonneville High School student, Ashlee Jyree Smith, died in a car wreck. Six years later a white cross and light purple and white flowers still mark the intersection where the accident happened. I look at Ashlee's name every time I stop at the intersection. I remember the day very well. February 23 was my friend Maryia's birthday. We had a lunch planned at Chinese Gardens. Just before leaving my house, I decided to take some oversized garbage to the Telford landfill, located north of Iona. After leaving the pit, as I came upon the Iona/Yellowstone intersection I could see a wreck had just happened. It looked really bad. I was bothered by the thought that someone may have died. I also had the unpleasant feeling that if I didn't do a better job making Vaughn stay in his seatbelt, the same thing may happen to me. I saw a teenage boy getting out of a wrecked car. Two police cars were at the scene. I could hear sirens of the on-coming fire truck and ambulance.

I drove past the wreck and pulled into the old Waremart grocery store parking lot, (I needed a birthday card). By the time I got out of the store I could see all the emergency vehicles at the intersection. For the rest of the day I was impressed there was a reason I had passed that way. I did not need to go to the dump that day. Two and a-half months later, Vaughn and Aisha passed away. I feel this incident is one small piece of our puzzle. As John Donne wrote, "God's hand is in every translation." I was being prepared.

Not just the obituaries but reading the whole newspaper is a constant reminder that none of us are ever alone on an island of grief. A mist of tears, sorrow, and anger often obscure the view of other islands; but they're out there, much closer than we realize, and people are on those islands, who have gone through horrible things and when we wade out in the water, we find that it's only ankle deep. Walking through the shallow water feels good and pulls the attention away from our own sadness. When coming ashore someone else's island, if you look around and listen, it's possible to forget about your own island--at least for a while.

John F. Kennedy Jr. and his fiancée also died in 1999. I was born the night his father President Kennedy was elected into office. I've always paid attention to and have read books about the Kennedys. They have suffered tremendous tragedies.

Within weeks of losing our kids we received our first newsletter from the Idaho Falls Chapter of The Compassionate Friends. The mission of The Compassionate Friends is to assist families toward the positive resolution of grief following the death of a child of any age and to provide information to help others be supportive. There are no religious ties or dues. The newsletter is accomplished through volunteer work. These kind people are deeply involved in mankind. They know for whom the bell tolls.

One day during the late summer of 1999 I was at the church cannery. A group of about six women were standing around a table filling boxes with canned food. After awhile, I briefly mentioned my tragedy to the group. After the boxing was done one of the women who had heard my story pulled me aside and introduced herself. Marsha later said I looked like I was on automatic survival mode. She felt a kinship and was impressed to help. (Marsha Nelson lost two daughters', Lisa 20 and Lacey 8, in a van / truck accident January 4, 1995. This accident also took the lives of Veniece Ricks 20, Trudi Tanner 19 and Shaun Dexter 17.)

A few weeks later, Marsha and I were pleasantly surprised to find each other enrolled in the same evening religion class. After a few of those classes we had time to talk. Around Christmas time Marsha brought to our house a tape of Daniel H. Ludlow's devotional talk on the resurrection. I've always believed in the resurrection but didn't know all the details Dr. Ludlow teaches. It all makes sense and has added tremendously to my testimony of Jesus Christ's atonement.

Someday when God binds up all his scattered leaves again for that library where every book shall lie open to one another, we will then discover all the remaining lost pieces to our life's puzzle.

(A copy of the devotional can be obtained by calling BYU-Idaho's bookstore, 208-496-2211, and ordering by phone or online at www.byuibookstore.com devotionals, Daniel Ludlow, March 14, 1995)

Chapter 11
The Miracle

___

David

Tomorrow would be the one-year anniversary of Vaughn's and Aisha's death. Tomorrow would be the day Linda was going to give birth to our son. I felt that some loving, unseen power was speaking to our hearts and a miracle was going to occur.

Linda was having contractions about a half hour apart when we went to bed.

Early the next morning they became a little more frequent and Linda's water broke. Her contractions were becoming more painful. I was up early. I went upstairs into the kitchen. There on the kitchen table was a fancy photo album and a pile of pictures. The cover was made of shiny white satin material, trimmed in lace. Framed and centered on the front cover of the album is a 5 x 7 Greg Olson Be Not Afraid picture. It shows Christ standing on rocks at the side of a flowing stream, holding a little boy in one arm and helping a little girl up onto a boulder by her right hand. The picture has a strong meaning to anyone who has lost children.

The Primary presidency went to a lot of work putting this album together. I sat down and looked at the pictures next to the album. Two photos, one of Vaughn and one of Aisha, caught my attention. They were at primary sitting on a table next to a picture of Jesus Christ. Under the pictures each child had a different scripture. Vaughn's picture read: "If ye have faith ye hope for things which are not seen, which are true" (Alma 32:21).

Aisha's scripture read: "And we believe and are sure that thou are that Christ, the Son of the living God." (John 6:69) I had never seen these photos before. That was remarkable considering how hungry I had been to see every picture of my children. We had asked friends and family to supply us with anything they had taken. I felt the spirit as I sat there at the table. I know that at that instant I was supposed to see these pictures, and not any earlier. Vaughn and Aisha were very literally speaking to me. They were testifying of Jesus Christ. They were telling me to believe in things unseen.

My heart was full. I cried as I felt them there with me. They remained with us through the rest of the day. Kelly Sorenson and her presidency had been inspired. Miracles, or at least a portion of them, come to pass through the inspiration and efforts of others. Sometimes those efforts can have long reaching effects that they are unaware of. To that primary presidency, thank you for being a part of our miracle.

Linda's contractions had stopped on the way to the hospital. I completed all the paperwork as Linda went on up to the maternity ward. They wanted to see if the labor was real. I met Linda upstairs and got the news: 4 centimeters. We went back down to fill out more paperwork. The clerk suggested Linda and I return home and come back later.

Linda and I looked at each other in disbelief. We both knew that Linda was going to have the baby today. We even knew that it would be around 2:25 PM. The few contractions that Linda had were no Braxton Hicks. Her labor had started. Her water had broken. It was May 11th. In the few moments Linda was upstairs talking to the nurse, she had related a few details about the loss of our two children one year ago today. Linda mentioned that she believed that it was significant that she was going to have her baby today.

The clerk downstairs was so sure Linda was going to go back home that she started filling out the paperwork that way. She called upstairs and talked to the nursing staff in the maternity ward. To her surprise they said Linda would be staying. We had no doubts the baby was coming today. The Spirit was telling us this. At 8:30 a.m. we went back upstairs to the maternity ward and got situated in one of the recovery rooms. I sat down in a recliner and Linda got comfortable on the bed. During the next few hours Linda's labor pains came back and became more regular.

Linda made some phone calls. We talked and waited. By 11:30 a.m. Linda's labor had increased and was getting harder and more regular. We were moved into the delivery room. Linda said to the nurse that she was a real "wimp" and wanted a spinal block to deaden the pain. After six births this would be Linda's first epidural. An anesthetist came in and prepared her needles.

We had been talking to the nursing staff about the incredible timing of this birth. Linda and I talked about how some of the nursing staff seemed to understand the significance of our story and others didn't. The anesthetist was a pretty woman who had a nice smile. She had Linda sit on the edge of the bed, open the back of her gown and hunch her shoulders down to expose the area in the spine were she intended to place the shunt.

As I watched, it was clear she was unaware of the miracle that was about to happen. She made several attempts at placing the shunt. She was having difficulty and looked up at me again as if to say "Don't doubt my ability; I'll get it." At about the fifth try I envisioned the insertion tool for the shunt scraping the bony sides of the vertebrae as it made its way into the spinal column and penetrated the membrane surrounding the spinal cord. The image in my head was too vivid. My head was dizzy and the room was going dark. I drooped my head down between my knees. I felt tingly all over. I knew I was about to pass out.

After a moment one of the nurses noticed my condition and said "Mr. Jamison, are you O.K?" I answered, "No, I feel faint." They took me to the recovery room where a kind nurse brought me a glass of cool orange juice. I realized that I had missed breakfast. Five minutes passed and I was amazed by how much better I felt. I went back into the delivery room where, to my relief, Linda's shunt had been successfully placed.

It was now after 1:00 p.m. We were pleased when Marie Ritchie walked into the delivery room. Marie is an excellent nurse and also a friend. She helped deliver Isaac, our fourth child. Linda said, "Oh boy, this couldn't be more perfect now." I felt as if some predefined set of events were unraveling before my eyes. There was a peaceful spirit in the delivery room that afternoon as we related the miraculous timing of the coming event to Marie. Marie immediately understood the significance.

Later I asked Marie about one of the other nurses we had related our story to. The nurse seemed confused by our story. Marie said at first she didn't get it but then caught on and was excited. Marie continued and said that the nurses out in the nursing station were all buzzing about it and were excited. I remember thinking that this is their job. It has got to take something very different to break the daily cycle of small miracles the nursing staff experiences regularly. Some of them remembered the story of Vaughn and Aisha passing away one year ago.

Linda's contractions became stronger and more frequent. Dr. Mortimer arrived, and we started getting serious about having a baby. The birthing room underwent a transformation. The bed transformed into a birthing bed. Lighting was changed. People scurried in and out in an orchestrated fashion. Something wonderful was about to happen. Into this excited scurry at exactly 2:14 pm, Jayden David Jamison was born.

I can't describe the feeling in that room. It was so powerful that I was left without the ability to deny the significance of what was happening. Jayden took his first breath and looked at me. I cried. I was holding a representation of life in my hands. Life in the exact same moment that only a year ago represented death and sorrow. Life that I knew was a blessing from above meant to help heal the hearts of two grieving parents. Life that was sent in its timing as a sign of the grand design of our Savior: In all death there is the promise of rebirth.

I have never felt a more complete closing of a circle of events as this. I knew this was a message to me. A testament from above that sealed my belief in a loving God who sent his son Jesus Christ to break the bands of death. A seal of approval that the course I had taken in studying the mercies of our savior, having hope in a resurrection and reunion with my children, was correct.

I felt this testimony being burned into every fiber of my being. The spirit in that delivery room was so powerful that it was numbing. I was primed from the earlier pictures that morning to believe in the unseen.

I could feel the presence of more than just Linda, myself, and the hospital staff. Vaughn and Aisha wanted to feel close to me. They wanted me to know that they were there. They were. Jayden is a very special friend of Vaughn and Aisha.

Linda

During my nine months of pregnancy I did not anticipate the baby being born on May 11. Of the six births' I had given so far, three of them were substantially early, two were on the due date and only Aisha was a week late (she remained sunny side up and wouldn't drop). I didn't think it was possible to go ten days overdue. I remember wishing he could be born on a significant day. Easter was in late April that year. This would have been significant, or April 6, an important LDS church history date would have been nice, or even May 1, my sister's birthday would have had meaning.

My May 1 due date came and went. Then I realized that my husband's graduation day, May 4, was almost here; so if I wanted to attend his graduation at the Colonial Theater (downtown Idaho Falls) I would have to hold out until after the fourth. David had been taking college classes towards his engineering degree for most of our married life. I'm really glad I didn't have to miss his graduation.

The next day, Thursday May 5, was my last appointment with Dr. Hall. Being five days overdue he said he'd let me go until Sunday, but if I hadn't started on my own by then, he wanted to induce labor. Otherwise, his motorcycles and family were leaving for Moab, Utah, on Monday and he wouldn't be here to deliver my baby.

Knowing it was a matter of convenience not safety that Dr. Hall wanted to induce labor, I simply ignored his instructions to call him Sunday morning.

Monday morning May 8 arrived, and I was still not in labor. I was glad I hadn't called Dr. Hall. I didn't want to be induced. If we were going to be blessed with a miracle birth I wanted it to happen naturally.

I have always gained a lot of weight during my pregnancies. I was well over 200 pounds, 218 to be exact, during those last three days of Jayden's pregnancy. There was very little I wanted to do or had the energy for.

I have heard my whole life that faith precedes the miracle so I decided to do what I could to increase my faith. I spent a lot of time reading scriptures and praying. (I had stopped going to the temple in mid-April when I became too fat for my temple dress.)

I knew a May 11 birth would help heal a lot of hearts, especially my mother's. My mom told me that she was praying specifically for her grandson to be born on May 11 as a sign to know if it was really Vaughn's and Aisha's time to go. Many people told me during those final hours that they were praying for our miracle. I felt their prayers. As my faith increased the closer we got to May 11, my constant prayer became, "If it be possible please let Jayden be born within the very hour of Vaughn's and Aisha's death."

Dr. Mortimer was on call and delivered Jayden. This pleased me as Mortimer had delivered Vaughn five years earlier. I wanted Dr. Mortimer to know of the miracle he was helping with.

For the first time in seven births I wanted an epidural. Having no experience on how to push the baby out, I wasted about twenty minutes before I caught on to how to push with no feeling. I've always felt that had I not had an epidural or if I had had any previous experience, Jayden's birth would have been even closer to the exact minute of Vaughn and Aisha's death.

Jayden David Jamison was born at 2:14 p.m. May 11, 2000, within the very hour of Vaughn and Aisha passing away at 1:37p.m. May 11, 1999. We consider the timing of Jayden's birth a miracle.

David blessed Jayden on Fast Sunday July 2, 2000. After giving Jayden his name, David then said: "You have been born a miraculous birth. Your birth testifies of Jesus Christ and you will continue to testify of Jesus Christ your entire life."

Camille's Birth

Jayden's May 11 birth however, does not end the good part of our story. Seventeen and a half months later, on the evening of October 25th I was sitting at our piano practicing primary songs while waiting for James and Laurie Browning to pick David and me up. We had a dinner date to Johnny Carino's in celebration of David's and James's 41st birthdays. (They were both born October 25th, 1960, in the same Idaho Falls Riverview Hospital. The same doctor, James Davis delivered both of them.)

I was nine months pregnant with our eighth child, who was due November fourth. Ten minutes before Browning's arrived my water started to leak. I immediately stopped practicing the piano and went downstairs to our master bathroom to tell David. He responded with a wink and a grin, and said, "You're not going to ruin my birthday are you?"

Having been through labor and delivery seven times before, KNOWING that my body takes forever to deliver a child, I decided I would try not to ruin the birthday party.

I took a hand towel off the bathroom shelf, and said, "Don't tell the Browning's." As the doorbell rang, I put on David's big coat. I was both happy and amused. Happy to have my miserable third trimester end and amused that it was all happening under such unusual circumstances.

By walking slowly and sitting very still I was able to make it through dinner. By the time we left the restaurant James and Laurie were informed of our secret. We drove two blocks to 17th Street, and I decided it made more sense to be taken to the hospital now while we were this close. Because we were with Browning's, David would need his own car. He helped check me in then went home with Browning's. Labor was slow starting. When contractions did pick up, it became apparent that our baby was in distress. With each contraction her heart rate dropped substantially. Sometime around midnight David and James came back to the hospital and gave me a blessing in which I was promised everything would be fine. Camille was born 21 hours later at 5:51 p.m. on October 26, 2001.

Even though I had an ultrasound on Camille, we did not need one to know this spirit coming to our home was going to be a girl. Twenty-three years ago during the spring of our first year of marriage, I had a dream in which I saw a girl who was about 14 years of age. She had blonde hair and blue eyes. The shape of her face was much like mine and her nose was definitely more like David's. I could feel a very dynamic personality coming from the girl. She was laughing a lot and had brightness of mind. I remember being happy about the dream. It reassured David and I that we would indeed have children. The girl's cheerful laughter took away my fear of having kids.

Our first child did not turn out to be this blue-eyed, blonde haired girl. Daniel is a brown-eyed, red head.

Dan's two sisters following him are equally red headed. I knew we still didn't have the girl in my dream when my next two sons were born, Isaac and Vaughn. Finally on May 10, 1996, I gave birth to a really blonde-haired girl. Even though Aisha's eyes were brown I was convinced this was the girl in my dream. When Aisha died the day after her third birthday, my dream no longer made sense. It was a fourteen-year old girl I saw.

A few months after Jayden's birth however, we began to feel the presence of another spirit. Jayden was eight months old when his little sister was conceived. During the entire nine months of the pregnancy, we always called her Camille. Her eyes are blue, and her hair is red! On Camille's second birthday Roslyn was combing Camille's hair and said, "Look how blonde Camille's hair is underneath." We believe Camille is the girl from my dream.

Courage Overcame Fear

David

I reflect back to a time prior to Jayden's birth. I had a keen awareness of the irreplaceable nature of our kids. My mind was full of doubts and questions. I found myself living in a different world. Raising children had become a risky business: one potentially fraught with tragedy and pain. Linda wanted more children. Could I find the courage to have more? It would be much easier to insure myself no more pain by just saying I'm through, and then never have another child. I was also afraid that people might misconstrue having more children as an attempt at directly replacing the ones we lost.

Pain and sorrow dictated, that to mourn, we should wear a sackcloth memorial by vowing to never have another child as long as we live.

I also feared that people would believe that we as grieving parents would force any new children into playing the roles of the children that we had lost. Something that the new children could never do and may even come to resent. As I reflected on these issues I thought of how clear the differences are between Daniel my oldest son and Isaac my second oldest son. Why should I be any more paranoid of a new arrival than Dan or Isaac, or my girls Sarah and Roslyn? I dearly love and value the individuality of each of them.

Somehow I found the courage to have more children. I am thankful that I did not allow these paranoid thoughts to win me over. Jayden and Camille were born and have blessed our lives in countless ways. Their presence has been the greatest healing part of our experience. I now realize that rejecting the love of children for the rest of my life based on paranoia or bereavement would have been wrong. It is clear that Jayden is not Vaughn and Camille is not Aisha. I will tell you who they are to us.

They are pure love.
They are happiness and joy.
They are life in our home that only a child's spirit can bring into the home.
They are noise and mischief, games and toys.
They are curiosity and children's play.
They surprise us with their intelligence
and humble us with their innocence.

They are abundant hugs and kisses when we need them more than they do.
They are energy released, messes laid behind a storm of play.
They try us when they fight, soothe us when they listen to bedtime stories and fall asleep in our arms.
They are peace and security tucked into bed, asleep under our watchful care.
They bless us with their presence.

In all of these things Jayden and Camille are direct replacements. These are the things only a child can bring into the home. These are things we apologize to no one for wanting in our home. These are things we are blessed to have in our home.

Chapter 12
Fire Reports

Linda

We learned many details about the fire, some of them the day after and some almost six years later when I obtained a copy of the fire report and the 911dispatch tape. The material campers are made out of is extremely flammable and toxic, especially foam mattresses. One breath of smoke coming from burning foam material is usually lethal. From the moment Vaughn struck the match igniting the foam mattress to the time the whole trailer was engulfed in flames was easily less than five minutes.

Kim Getsinger, Captain of Engine #3, explained the principal of back draft: When fire starts in an enclosed room, oxygen is quickly used up. With no air to help the fire burn, it smolders. Incomplete combustion occurs, producing a lot of black smoke. The longer the incomplete combustion continues the more superheated the interior of the enclosed room becomes. Then, if and when oxygen is introduced into the enclosed room, everything wants to burn all at once. In other words, an explosion occurs.

Kim told me that when I opened the back camper door the conditions were such that a back draft explosion could have and probably should have occurred. Like most house fires, the temperature of our camper fire was at least 1800 degrees. The moment I opened the camper door the internal temperature was already 1300 degrees. The neighbors green grass next to the haystack burned, and the tractor inside the barn melted. It's a good thing that Miles and David did not complete the previous summer's project of replacing the chain link fence with solid wood cedar planks. Had that wooden fence caught fire, it would have ignited their entire house.

Vaughn's body was located in the northeast corner, directly below where the overhang would have been. Aisha's body was found in the opposite southwest corner. All of the debris toward the front of the camper had slightly more burn damage and charring than the rear of the camper. This burn pattern was probably affected by the wind coming from the southwest.

As graphic as some of these after-the-fact details are, they are important. If the reader understands the positions of where Vaughn and Aisha's bodies were found, then the reader will immediately understand the accuracy and importance of Aunt Marilyn's dream.

Aunt Marilyn's Dream

Early Tuesday morning May 11, David's Aunt Marilyn had a dream, which foreshadowed the tragedy, which would occur that afternoon. In the dream Marilyn, who represents me, had some kind of tool in her hand and was doing yard work. (I had been removing accumulated grass from around the lawnmower blade with a chisel.) Next in the dream are two children, a boy and a girl. The boy is older. (Vaughn and Aisha) The boy and girl are in some kind of rectangular box-like structure that sits low to the ground. (The floor of the camper-, which is where the fire started.)

Suddenly a large, golden-yellow mountain lion comes charging towards Marilyn and the two children. The lion is extremely frightening with its flared-out mane and huge rippling muscles that quiver in constant motion. As the lion (fire) rushes toward the children inside the box, the frightened little boy scrambles "up and away," onto a high, cliff-like place. The little girl scrambles "down and away" in the opposite direction of the boy.

Marilyn tried to get the kids to come to her. She couldn't go after them. Marilyn said, "You've got to come with me, or I can't save you." They wouldn't come. The little boy sat calmly and looked at Marilyn as if confused by her panic and said, "What's wrong? It's okay lady, don't worry, we're going."

At this point in the dream Marilyn awoke with fright. She knew the two children were not her grandkids; their gender and ages did not match.

Dreams of this type have happened to Marilyn before. Once she had a dream about her Uncle Adrian and was able to describe certain things about the funeral before it happened. On the day her own father died, Marilyn experienced chest pains so severe that her husband Travis almost took her to the hospital. Her father was killed in a truck-automobile collision that crushed his chest. Dreams of this nature have only involved people Marilyn is related to. All of them have foreshadowed death.

Years Later

David

Now, years later as I have had time to look at more of the puzzle pieces that Linda referred to earlier and after hearing the fire report, several things came to mind that I feel I need to share. I will go back to the day immediately following the accident. May 12, 1999.

The firemen came in the door and asked if they could talk to Linda and me. There were people around the house, and it was obvious that they wanted to talk to us in private. We decided to go to a back bedroom. I remember four or five people cramming into the small bedroom for privacy. There the firemen asked important questions about the fire. They had specific questions. It was obvious that they were puzzled about the speed with which the camper shell had burned after catching fire. We answered each question the best we could. They asked me to remember everything that was in the camper.

I recalled placing a heavy marble slab over the vent hole in the roof after the wind had caught the plastic cover and torn it off. It was heavy and there was no way it would blow away. I went into the camper and discovered that the foam mattress in the area that extends above the truck cab was soaking wet with rain that came through the vent hole I had just covered. I removed the mattress and hung it over a chain link fence at the back of the camper to dry. They asked very specific questions about this foam mattress. I answered them as best I could, explaining that it was an egg crate type foam mattress in very poor condition.

The questioning was over and they were about to leave when I said, "Is it ok if I ask a few questions?" They looked surprised and said yes. I, too, was concerned about how fast things had burned and asked if the kids might have turned the gas stove on. They answered that the knobs on the stove were in the off position. I then asked if it were possible that one of the propane tanks ignited, burning things faster. They said that they had looked at that, too. The tanks had a relief mechanism that had actually melted open due to the extreme heat, but the insides of the container that the tanks sat in had no charring, indicating that the tanks were completely empty at the time the fire occurred.

The next day they returned and had more questions. They asked to talk to the whole family. We gathered the family together into the front room. They went around the room and asked each of our kids if they had seen anything in the camper. To our amazement the kids reported that a neighbor boy remembered looking in there with one of them once and saw strike tip matches scattered around on the floor of the camper. I was terrified at this revelation.

They were about done when they asked if there were anything else in the camper. I remember thinking hard and trying to remember any details but it had been months since I had been in the camper. I related everything I could remember about removing the mattress from the camper. The mattress sat on the fence for a while, but it was in such poor shape that it started to fall apart and we threw it away.

Then it got to Roslyn and she was asked what she had recently seen in the camper. At first I thought I heard her say, "I saw matches." I blurted out, "You saw matches!" I was about to get angry at not having been informed about the matches. Roslyn turned her head around quickly and said, "No. I saw a mattress." With this I was speechless. I thought hard for a few seconds and it came to me that there were two mattresses. I had hung one over the chain link fence and the other one I left in the camper shell. I placed it upright in the aisle way, standing it on its narrowest end to dry out. I left it there leaning on the refrigerator to dry. I passed all this information on to the firemen. They were satisfied. I later found that they were very thorough and questioned my Dad about the contents of the camper shell as well. He verified my story about having two mattresses stored in the over the cab section of the camper shell.

Years later as Linda was given the fire reports and we prepared to write this story several more pieces of the puzzle fell into place. The fire report mentioned that the charring toward the front of the camper was much deeper and more severe than toward the rear of the camper. It immediately became clear to me why this was so. This area was above the spot where I had placed the mattress. Foam mattresses are extremely flammable.

An improbable sequence of events leads up to this accident. I found that I was implicated in that chain of events. Anywhere along the way an intervention could have broken the chain. We never can tell when some seemingly benign act we perform can actually set the stage for an accident. I was recently watching a safety video at work of a Christmas tree fire. Within two minutes the room the tree was in was dark from ceiling to floor with pitch-black smoke. It happened so fast that anyone in that home would have been in extreme danger. Seconds later a temperature known as the flashover point was reached and all the contents of the room began to burn spontaneously. I compare the speed of that burning Christmas tree to the speed of an upright foam mattress sitting on its end in the aisle of the camper.

Linda truly was surprised by how rapidly the camper burned. Literally, one minute our kids were healthy and playing and the next minute they were gone. There is nothing she could have done.

All these years I have wondered why an intervention could not have occurred to save the lives of my kids. I never focused on the intervention that did occur to save the life of my wife, Linda. Had she entered the camper I would have lost her, too. I am thankful for that voice that said, "Stay out! You have four more children to raise." I am thankful for my wife Linda.

Chapter 13
Our Children Write

Dan was a seventh grader at Rocky Mountain Middle School the day of our tragedy. When Maryia called the middle school to have Dan ready to be picked-up a student body assembly was in session.

Dan

The bleachers were really packed. Jesse, Evan and I were sitting up high. I watched a lady walking down on the gym floor past everyone. She stopped directly below us and motioned for me to come down. There was confusion on who she meant. I was surprised she wanted me. I went down and followed her out of the gym. When we got close to the office the lady told me there had been an emergency and that my mom's friend was coming to get me. While waiting on the white bench in front of the office I thought, "I wonder if someone died?"

When Maryia came her eyes were red, as we walked down the hall she put her arm around me. When she started to cry, I started to cry because I knew something bad was coming before she told me. I couldn't believe it, "How can they be dead?" I thought. When we got in the car I asked Maryia, "Are you sure they're dead?"

A few weeks later while in history class I was handed a slip to go to counseling. Six other kids were there. We were told that, "Every kid in this room has had a significant loss. We are offering a counseling session." Then they told us about it.

I thought it was stupid to miss a class for this. I didn't want to get behind in history. Your family is so much more important than any councilor, just the comforting you get at home. Grandpa Smith was there; he helped me a lot. I felt comforted. It's time that heals, to be able to talk about it and not cry. A couple of nights I cried when I went to bed. When relatives came and cried it made me cry.

Mom said that you can pray to be comforted by the Holy Ghost and it will help--even during the day at school. I did and it helped.

The biggest thing about Jayden's birth to me was my mom praying for Jayden to be born on a certain day. It was a big testimony to see that prayers are answered.

Kids at school who said, "Didn't your brother and sister die?" were super annoying, if they talked about it in front of a class audience. One kid asked me about it alone and seemed very sincere. I appreciated that. An English teacher, Mrs. Waetje, had the whole class write sympathy notes; that made me feel good.

Sarah

I thought Mom would be mad at me for forgetting my lunch for our 5th grade field trip. When she poked her head in Mrs. Barrie's classroom she was smiling. She handed me my lunch in the blue INEEL lunch bag my dad got from his work.

I remember eating lunch on the grass with my friend Lara. It was nice weather.

We went into a big building, up some stairs and down a hall into the cadaver lab at Ricks College (now BYU

Idaho). Everyone circled around the center cadaver and the professor. It was hard to hear because of the vent fans directly over our heads. If these weren't there, the formaldehyde smell would be overpowering. They didn't let us see the cadaver's face. I was very interested and listened intently for over half the presentation. When the professor got to the lungs he had us feel the difference between a human lung and a pig lung. The pig lung looked and felt like styrofoam. I thought this was neat. Shortly after I felt the pig lung an overwhelming sad feeling came over me. There was nothing to be sad about. I tried to focus in again. I tried to listen and concentrate on what the instructor was saying next but felt my eyes tearing up and my face getting red hot. I even stepped back so no one would notice, but this didn't work. Mrs. Barrie asked if I was okay. I nodded and tried to suck it up and remain quiet. This sort of worked but after another minute of not being able to concentrate or calm down I knew I had to leave.

I walked quickly to the big, brown, heavy door. I started walking down the hall crying harder now. I didn't know what was wrong or what to do. Other kids had left the cadaver lab, but I didn't know where they had gone. As I was walking, a college girl walked down the hall towards me. She stopped and tried to comfort me. I was crying so hard now I couldn't stop long enough to get more than a few words out before the next spout came. I was embarrassed of my lack of self-control. I felt bad because the girl had no idea what I was doing there or what was wrong. Once I got it out that I didn't know what was wrong, she must have been really confused. She had me sit down against the wall.

Mrs. Barrie came out and saw us. The entire other fifth grade class walked right by us three. I was so embarrassed. Soon I was walking with Mrs. Barrie. She put her arm around me. I could hardly talk. She gave me a piece of double mint gum. It helped. We walked up and down the stairs. I finally got myself under control so I could actually talk. Mrs. Barrie questioned me, but I had no answer to why I was sad or what was wrong.

I felt better after a little while and didn't think much about this incident until a few days later.

When we got back to Fairview, it was time to go home. Janie, the secretary, called the Jamison kids to the office over the intercom and told us not to ride the bus home. Isaac, Roslyn and I waited in the teachers' lounge sitting on a brown plaid couch. Mrs. Barrie came in later after the bell rang. She was happy but I sensed something was different with her. I figured we had a dentist appointment or piano lessons. Eileen Adams came.

At the Roberts house we all cried hard at the news. I felt numb. After Mom broke the news to us, I said "No" sort of loud and put my face in my hands and cried. I remember feeling embarrassed after I said "no" wishing I hadn't. There was a box of tissues being passed around. I was annoyed when it kept coming to me. I didn't want everyone to watch me. Kathy McBride was sitting next to me. She started lightly scratching my back. I was glad she was there, and I could feel her love.

The feeling I remember having most was tremendous love from everybody. Having our extended family there helped the most. Grandma Jamison hugged me for an eternity. I still remember her grandma smelling perfume. I didn't always know how to act or what to say. Mom and Dad talked a lot to every one there. I learned a lot from listening to them and the positive things they had to say. Kayla Smith came. I was excited to be in Young Women's because she would be my teacher. She always has something nice to say and makes a person laugh. It felt so good to be cheered up. Mom said she was grateful for Kayla's comic relief.

My grade school best friend, Lara came over. I was glad for her support. We split a big poppy seed muffin warmed in the microwave and drank some milk. Our island in the kitchen was filled with food. I wasn't the least bit hungry. A lot of people told us kids we needed to eat even if we didn't feel like it. Crying takes a lot out of you.

That first night reality was starting to sink in. Upstairs my mom's friend Tracy said a prayer with us kids, now four of us. This was very comforting, and I was glad for the spirit it brought. I wasn't used to not having to get a toddler brother or sister in pajamas. I thought it would be hard to sleep but I went out fast. I had a peaceful feeling.

That first morning I heard a pitter-patter of little feet running on the hard wood floor down stairs. Mom said she heard it too. Isaac was up, but Vaughn and Aisha weren't running around with him.

Friends and family were the biggest help. Another friend Heather brought over a card and a cute bear from my soccer team. Mary, my friend Marissa's mom, came the second night with blueberry muffins Marissa helped her make. She said a prayer with me in my room and even tucked me in bed.

There were always so many people at our house. Sometimes I wanted it to be just our family. The people showed us we were loved and cared about. Listening mostly to my parents, talking to friends and family, and time helped me through.

Roslyn

May 11, 1999. It was almost time for the bell to ring, so my third grade class and I were putting our chairs on top of our desks and getting our backpacks ready to take home. It had been a good day and we had just finished practicing our crocheting. I was holding a spring colored miniature basket I crocheted. Mrs. Reed had been teaching us how to make hot pads. I never understood how to make one right. Every time I tried to change directions and start a new row it hardly ever worked. That's why I decided to make a basket because I could crochet in one continuous circle without having to change directions. I wanted to give the basket to Aisha.

The bell rang. Instead of going to the buses I waited in the teacher's lounge with Sarah and her teacher Mrs. Barrie. Someone announced that we were supposed to wait for our mom to come get us. We waited for a long time, and I started to get bored.

Mrs. Barrie was talking to us and asked what we had done that day. The biggest thing we did was make atom-models out of brightly colored marshmallows and toothpicks. I showed the model to her and explained that it was an atom. After Mrs. Barrie talked to us we waited some more and I decided to eat the marshmallows from my model. Mrs. Reed had told us not to because they had been handled before. I didn't care. They looked good enough to eat, and so I ate them.

We were playing pool when my mom came through the game room door with my oldest brother Daniel following right behind. Both of them had red eyes. I walked up to them and asked, "What Happened?" My mom walked past me and didn't respond. I resorted to Daniel and asked, "What happened!" He didn't want to answer and shook his head no, then also walked past me.

Then my mom told us kids to come sit down on the couches. I sat down and started fidgeting with my yarn basket. Mom and Daniel's red eyes made me nervous. I kept having random thoughts. I looked down at my crocheted basket I was holding and thought, "I won't give this to Aisha. It's pretty weird looking, and it's so small she wouldn't be able to put anything in it.

The next moment I heard my mom take a deep breath and then said, "There's been a fire. Vaughn and Aisha were in it, and they're dead." I pictured Vaughn in his blue shirt from Hawaii and all I could think was, "Gone? How?" Things like this happen, but not to us...

I didn't know what to think.

My mom had looked each of us in the eyes. I knew they were dead. I was sad, and I started crying after Sarah yelled out, "No!" I felt shaky and I started playing with my yarn basket again. Other people from our neighborhood had come, and I didn't want them to see me crying. I was a little bit self conscious, but I knew it was okay to be crying because everyone else was crying too.

After crying for a while Maryia told someone to go get the kids a drink of water. When only four large red cups were brought back I thought it was a small number compared to six.

I got up to get one of the cups. I wasn't thirsty, but it was something to do. There were a lot of people in that game room. Under normal circumstances I would have felt extremely shy and self-conscious, but instead I felt a sense of peace. My shaky feeling left, and I felt calm when an older woman gave me a hug. I don't remember who she was, but I felt loved.

When we left the Roberts' house, Sarah and I rode back to our house with my Aunt Anita and cousin Becky Burke. Anita talked to us. It felt good just to be talking with some family members. I felt my sense of calm grow stronger into a feeling of comfort. I knew everything was okay, even though Vaughn and Aisha had just died. The Spirit was very warm and comforting to me that day. It helped me see past death and know that having loved ones on the other side isn't bad at all. I knew that families can truly be together forever.

Isaac

After we got into Adams car I saw Eileen look sideways. She had a sad and worried expression. I was confused and quite a bit worried myself. The ride to Robert's house seemed long because of the silence.

After my mom told us Vaughn and Aisha were dead many people burst into tears. I remember feeling sad but did not start crying until I saw my brother and two sisters sobbing. I guess that when I cried I looked cute because lots of the people in the room wanted to hold me and hug me. I was passed around from one sobbing person to the next.

Chapter 14
Tears to Triumph

When Maggie Walsh, a Post-Register journalist, came to our house to interview David and I she said she could get us as many extra copies of the story as we needed. As it turned out Maggie had to scramble and secured only six. People were coming into the Post Register off the streets requesting extra copies. Ten months later I saw Maggie in Albertsons. In the conversation she mentioned that many people had inquired about our family. Knowing of this reader interest has been a large part of our motivation to write. As a community Idaho Falls was very compassionate. We received cards, letters and plants from people we didn't even know. My neighbor, Debbie told me that one of the local radio stations (KUPI) did a one-minute silence in recognition of our children. I was touched. Fairview elementary cancelled the Thursday evening, family reading night, in respect of the Jamison family. We thank you all. I hope our book finds all those people who want to know the rest of our story.

Mother's Day Article 2001

TEARS TO TRIUMPH

Mother finds hope, 'no matter what happens'

By MAGGIE HALL WALSH
Post Register

It's been a bittersweet week for Linda and David Jamison.

Thursday would have been Aisha's fifth birthday.

Friday was the second anniversary of the fire.

And the day Jayden turned 1.

So, on Thursday the family visited the cemetery. They went back again on Friday and placed flowers and toy animals--a squirrel for Vaughn, a rabbit with a hair bow for Aisha--on the children's graves.

Linda spent two hours in the LDS temple, where she feels closest to the dead.

Then it was time to celebrate Jayden and somehow put the last 24 months into perspective.

The Jamison's know all about heartbreak. And how to savor the joys that come with parenthood.

ISAAC

They remember the day, years ago, when they nearly lost Isaac at the Green Canyon pool. Linda remembers the shock of realizing the 3-year-old was missing. "Where is Isaac?" she hollered at David, in that panicky moment every parent dreads. David shrugged her off. "He's around here somewhere. Maybe he's in the bathroom."

She relaxed for a few seconds, and then stiffened, stood up, and screamed, "DAVID! WHERE IS ISAAC?"

This time, David started searching and saw Linda wade through a pool full of splashing children to pluck up Isaac, floating unconscious six inches below the surface of the water.

David breathed life back into the boy, amazed that some unseen hand had guided Linda across the pool, directly to Isaac. "I know what it is to save a child," said Linda. "I know what it is to receive divine intervention. That's what that was."

Linda and David believe the hand of God works in mysterious ways, ways in which the child isn't always saved.

VAUGHN AND AISHA

May 11, 1999, was a lovely, breezy spring day. The older children were at school, their father was at work and the two little ones and their mom were at their country home northwest of Idaho Falls. The three spent the morning doing chores, sanding the outside deck, reading books, and snacking on peaches and homemade bread.

Vaughn was a serious 4-year-old who chose his words carefully and once yelled at a workman who was remodeling the kitchen for knocking holes in the walls. He had two older sisters, two older brothers and a little sister who was his best friend. He spent hours drawing pictures of cars and had heard his favorite book, Dr. Seuss' "ABC" so many times that he had it memorized.

Aisha had just turned 3. Nicknamed Ladybug, she learned to talk early and was known to sneak up on family members to tickle and tease them. Aisha lived to play with her dolls and jumped at any chance to be wrapped in a blanket and rocked on her mama's lap.

At about 1:40 in the afternoon, Linda was on the driveway, cleaning grass out of the lawnmower blade. The children had been playing nearby in the yard, where a truck-top camper was being stored. Linda didn't like the children to play in the camper, but she knew it was irresistible to them. She would later learn the older children had seen matches on the camper's floor.

Aisha's scream jolted Linda. She looked up, to see oily black smoke in the window of the camper. "There was a 30-foot high plume of smoke above the camper. It was consumed in flames. I ran over and opened the back door…smoke came out at me. It was unreal how much there was," Linda said. "My first thought was the water hose. I thought, "That's not going to work; it's too far away.' I remember screaming. I was helpless, completely helpless."

What happened next has played over and over in Linda's mind for two years. Although others judged her, she says she knows she did the right thing.

"I had a sudden thought. It wasn't a voice; it was just a clear thought. In the panic and terror and horror of it all, it was the only clear thought I had: "Leave them alone. You have four other children to raise," she said.

A member of the Church of Jesus Christ of Latter-day-Saints, Linda believes God was protecting her from the toxic smoke that filled the camper. "We believe in the Holy Ghost. We believe it was the Holy Ghost prompting me," she explained. "There are people who are LDS that would believe this and understand. There are people of other faiths who will understand and believe, and I'm sure there are people who will scoff at it."

Linda ran to the phone and called 911. "The whole thing was engulfed in flames. I stood there and screamed, 'My children are in there! I couldn't get them. I knew they were dead," she said.

David says that if he had been with the children that day he would have ignored the smoke and tried to enter the camper to reach the children. Linda believes that if that had been the case, she would not only have lost the children but her husband as well. But David never blamed Linda for the children's deaths.

"There really is no such thing as an accident," he said. "Our children were taken, and they were taken for a reason. We just don't know what that reason is. Their deaths are not meaningless."

The memory of Isaac's near-drowning at Green Canyon is enough proof for David that some things are out of the hands of mere humans. "I saw Linda react immediately when Isaac was gone, even when I didn't believe there was a problem," he said. "I watched her walk right to his body. She was guided to save him. If I hadn't seen how strongly she reacted (that day), I might have blamed her for (Vaughn and Aisha's) deaths. I know there was nothing she could have done.

JAYDEN

Three months after the children's deaths, in the midst of the family's mourning and just as the loss of Vaughn and Aisha was really sinking in, Linda discovered she was pregnant.

She and David were elated. "When they died, the children were at my favorite stage, 3 and almost 5," she said. "I just really needed another child; there was such a void. This baby was not to replace the other two--you can never replace a child--but it just helped fill the void."

"Doctors set her due date at May 1 and since the other children were either born early or on their due dates-except Aisha, who arrived a week late-Linda expected to give birth in late April. Her due date came and went. The doctor wanted to induce labor, but she refused. "I wanted it to be natural," she said.

On the evening of May 10, 2000, as the memories of the next day's sorrowful anniversary settled over the family, Linda began the early stages of labor.

They'd been through labor enough to realize that there was no need to rush to the hospital at the first sign of contractions, so Linda and David spent the night awake at home, keeping each other company. In the early morning of May 11, as David was paging through the family's photo albums, he came across two photos of Vaughn and Aisha he had never seen before.

The photos had been taken two months before their deaths during Primary, their church's Sunday school time, and depicted each child seated before a painting of Jesus and a scripture verse.

The verse behind Aisha reads: "And we believe and are sure that thou are that Christ, the Son of the living God." In Vaughn's photo the verse reads: "If ye have faith, ye hope for things which are not seen, which are true."

David said he was deeply moved by the photos and accepted them as a sign. "I felt like they were sending us a message. I knew the baby would be born the same day they died," he said.

That afternoon, at 2:14 p.m., one year and 34 minutes after Vaughn and Aisha died, Jayden David Jamison was born.

"The feeling inside that delivery room was disbelief," recalled David. "We didn't actually see Vaughn and Aisha in the delivery room, but we definitely felt them. We feel the message they were trying to tell us was, 'We're here, Mom and Dad. We'll see you again.'"

It's difficult for Linda to sort out her feelings about May 11. She knows it always will be.

Two weeks before his first birthday, she found herself planning a big party for Jayden with lots of friends and balloons. "I thought,

'No, that doesn't feel right,'" she said. "Yes, we have reason to celebrate, but it's also their death day."

During the past two years Linda and David have relied heavily on friends and the example of other parents who have lost children to cope with their loss. Even people she doesn't know have given Linda strength, like a woman who approached her mother shortly after the fire and told her she'd had a dream about the fire. "In her dream, the children's spirits were removed very quickly," Linda said. "They felt no pain. That comforted me a great deal." And she has learned a valuable lesson about family and love and her own strength.

"No matter how bad of a tragedy life might hand you, there is no reason to give up. There's so much reason for hope and faith," she said. "You can be happy no matter what happens to you."

But it has been Jayden, the red-headed, blue-eyed baby of the family, that has given Linda and her family the most comfort and made them realize how unbreakable the circle of life is.

"The fact that I conceived, well, that's obviously not a miracle, but the timing of his birth is definitely a miracle," Linda said of Jayden. "He represents death and rebirth. These children died, they were taken, but they will live again. Jayden represents life."

As he cuddled his little boy on his lap, David quietly agreed with his wife. "He is what's taken a bad day and made it a good day."

Epilog

Daniel (19) is serving a LDS mission in San Francisco, California.

Dan is a talented percussionist. After his mission he plans to continue his education to become a Professor of Music. The marimba is his specialty.

Dan is also an avid tele-mark skier and mountain biker. He has a great personality and sense of humor.

Sarah (17) our oldest daughter has always had an excitement for life. When Sarah was little we lived at Smith Manor. When the day's first light filled the big old rooms of our three-story residence, Sarah, with great excitement, would often announce, "Mom, it's morning time, it's morning time!

Sarah enjoys many things like singing and piano, snowboarding and mountain biking.

Sarah is involved in health occupations and wants to become a health care professional.

Roslyn (15) is an artist. If I need an opinion on how something looks (like a landscape arrangement or a scrapbook page layout) Roslyn is the first one I ask. As a child she was the nature kid who gathered pinecones and twigs and made them into dolls.

Roslyn plays the piano and violin. She is an excellent water-skier. She can almost hold the rope with her foot.

Like her brother Dan, Roslyn does not lack a sense of humor.

Isaac (13) Up until two weeks before Isaac was born we were undecided on his name. I liked the name Taylor but David didn't. I received strong promptings that Taylor was not the right name and began searching through our genealogy books. When seeing a picture of Isaac and Elizabeth Smith we instantly knew Isaac was to be our son's name. Like his great-great-great grandfather, Isaac has a strong likeable personality; he's very talkative. Isaac is a well-rounded kid who reads a lot and is willing to try new things. This fall he ran cross-country for the first time and loves it! His passion is ballroom dancing.

Jayden (5) is in kindergarten at Fairview Elementary. Jayden seems smart to me. I don't know if that's because I'm his mother and I think all my kids are smart; or that we really have been blessed with an extraordinary child. He has an incredible sense of direction and is acutely observant. Jayden does a constant motor humming sound when he plays with his cars.

Camille (3) is pure affectionate sweetness. Everyday, many times throughout the hours my baby girl is on my lap or behind my back hugging my neck, and kissing my cheeks. She loves everything pretty and feminine. Fiona is her favorite princess. All dolls and real people who are dressed in pretty dresses are "Princesses" according to Camille. Usually on Sunday mornings Camille will take notice of what I am wearing and say," "Mom, you look like a princess!" Camille sings a lot while playing and loves to be read to.

Grandpa and Grandma Smith are enjoying retirement. They both turned 71 this summer of 2005. Mom is diligent in fighting her heart problem. Everyday she lifts hand weights and does a series of calisthenics, drinks eight glasses of water and takes her pills. She'll probably live to ninety. In the summers she does a load of yard work.

Dad reads a lot and attends the library book club. He likes to build birdhouses; some of them are more like bird hotels. And most of all Grandpa and Grandma Smith like to come out to my house and get loves and kisses from Jayden and Camille.

Grandpa and Grandma Jamison have kept busy with church work. They are currently serving their third mission. Their first mission eight years ago was in Little Rock, Arkansas. Next they served in Salt Lake City at the genealogical library. They are now fulfilling a third mission locally at the Idaho Falls family history center.

Our four oldest kids have had the good fortune of having Grandma Rosalie as their piano teacher. And much to my advantage she comes out to our house to teach! Jayden calls Rosalie, "Sweetheart Grandma."

Holly Dickinson (27) is a young lady from Basin, Wyoming who came to live with us eight years ago. We remodeled our home extensively to accommodate Holly's needs. She was born with spina bifida and uses a wheelchair. Since moving out to Coltman (north Idaho Falls) twelve years ago we have been care providers for adult developmentally disabled women.

Holly loves to watch professional sports on television, especially baseball. The Braves are her favorite. She has a bigger collection of sport cards than anyone I know.

Holly and I share the hobby of putting together picture puzzles. When the jigsaws are completed we brush mod-podge over the front. Holly's Uncle Harold builds picture frames for our puzzles. Many of them are hanging on our walls, some even in the garage.

During October of 2003 I started to receive strong promptings to write this story. After six weeks of trying I became discouraged. I started putting puzzles together with Holly as a distraction. David was disgusted and told me I was wasting a lot of time. He was right. We put together at least ten 500 to 1000 piece puzzles. I used the excuse that I was being a good care provider spending all that time with Holly. Trouble was that long after Holly went to bed and during the day while she was at school (Options) I would spend hours working her puzzles.

I did come to know puzzles and recognize that in many ways life is like putting one together. Every jigsaw and every human life is very different. Interlocking edges (religion) are important if you don't want your picture to come apart. Some puzzles are so tightly connected that the whole thing can be picked up before gluing and it won't separate. Some puzzles really do come from the factory with sections (meaningful life experiences) already put together. I use to think it was cheating not to pull the sections apart before I started. I now see them as blessings and record them in my journal.

When first starting a puzzle, if I take the time to be organized by turning all the pieces right side up and separating the edge and section pieces then the whole experience (daily life) goes much faster (more accomplishment in less time) and with less frustration.

Always when I stand up and have good lighting (proper equipment for the task at hand) and move my hands at a constant steady pace (take action, have faith even though the next step is not always known) the pieces (answers) seem to almost fall into place. But when I become discouraged and just sit and stare at the pieces nothing happens except a huge waste of time.

David is an engineer-scientist at the INL Electric Vehicle battery lab. He is currently enrolled in his first class towards a Master's Degree in nuclear engineering. Everyday he rides his Victory Motorcycle to work. During his lunch hour David swims a mile at the aquatic center. He looks as good as when we were twenty-five. During the summers he oversees our kids' pipe moving in our potato field next to our house. One night in August, Sarah, Roslyn and I took off to Rexburg with my cousin Lori. We said we would be back in time to move the pipe but weren't. David had to move most of the pipe himself with some help from our neighbor, Cody. When we got home it was dark and David was still out in the field fixing things. The girls and I thought he would be really mad. He wasn't. David is a 'Prince of a Fellow' just like his Grandpa Jamison.

Linda I am very glad to be done writing this book. The whole process has been highly educational and therapeutic. Many times I have cried. A closure has occurred that I didn't know I needed.

It is Wednesday August 25, 2005, Jayden's first day of kindergarten. It is almost time for Jayden to arrive home on his first school bus ride. I am sitting on the front porch with great anticipation. It is a warm day and the sun is shining bright. Jayden and Camille are now old enough to start doing the things we missed out on with Vaughn and Aisha.

There is Jayden now walking or rather skipping into our yard. As Jayden trots across the grass, Camille, who has been waiting with me, runs down the ramp with outstretched arms. As our two little angels embrace, Jayden says to Camille, "Did you miss me?"